JOURNEY FITNESS

Jeremy,
Hope my Journey
inspires yours!

[signature]

JOURNEY FITNESS

More Than Fitness. It's
Lives Touching Lives

BY TRAVIS BARNES WITH CYNDY BARNES
Foreword by Todd Durkin

ISBN: 1505595797
ISBN 13: 9781505595796

TABLE OF CONTENTS

FOREWORD BY TODD DURKIN

"Fear, frustration, and failure are overcome with faith, focus, forward-thinking, and follow-through!"

--WAYNE COTTON

Have you ever been so blind-sided by one's story that is stops you dead in your tracks?

Likewise, have you ever wondered how people not only survive the depths of despair, but then turn it all around and end-up wildly successful and IMPACTFUL?

For many years, I have preached that "Everyone has a life worth telling a story about...what's your story?"

I truly believe that there is greatness in everyone but that we must often overcome much fear, failure, frustration, rejection, challenge, adversity, pain, strife, challenge, or obstacle to really find our true path, passion, and purpose in life.

And I have always said that adversity, obstacles, and challenges can do one of 3 things to you:

1. They can knock you down to your knees, keep you down, and spiral you into a deep, dark place.
2. They can ultimately propel you forward by you choosing to DO SOMETHING positive with your life.
3. Or they can do both!

What would you choose?

As a performance coach, trainer, speaker, and business owner, I have had the opportunity to work with many "high level" athletes and executives. From NFL MVP's, Super Bowl champions & MVP's, MLB & NBA All-Stars, and Olympic Gold Medalists to the uber-successful entrepreneur that is worth millions of dollars.

And one thing is common with the great ones. All the ones I know and have worked with have overcome some form of adversity in their life. Major injury. Disease. Bankruptcy. Divorce. Tragedy in the family. Horrible childhood. Failed businesses. And the list goes on and on.

Now I am NOT saying you have to experience "tragedy" to be successful in life. You don't.

But here is the bottom line. "Good things" and "bad things" are going happen in life. And there are some things you can control and there are some things you can't control.

And a mantra I live by is, "It's not what happens TO us in life that counts. It's what we choose to DO with it that matters most."

Let me introduce to you Mr. Travis Barnes. He epitomizes all of the above. He has an incredible story and in the pages ahead, demonstrates incredible courage, faith, belief, and love as he shares his STORY.

I first met Travis at a Perform Better fitness conference in Providence, RI, in 2011. He was with his lovely wife Cyndy and about 5 of his teammates. He was tremendously respectful, you could tell he and his wife had a great love for each other, and there was admirable mutual respect between him and his teammates.

But even then, I didn't know the whole story.

You see, many people know Travis Barnes the trainer. The standout coach who transforms lives in his 2 up-state New York training studios (Journey Fitness). They know the Travis who opened a business in 2013, leads a solid team of trainers and fitness pros, and has found great success in helping people transform their lives. They know the Travis who is full of unbridled passion, deep commitment and dedication, and who has genuine concern, care, and love for all he touches.

And these are all the reasons WHY he is great at what he does.

But there is more.

Very few people knew of Travis' JOURNEY before this book. Or before he started his business.

This book shares the remarkable story how Travis Barnes' overcame 8.5 years of incarceration. And his never-ending hope and conviction to turn his life around. For his wife. For his daughter. For himself. And for his future.

As you read it, seek to understand, not to judge. Read intently and empathize. And realize that the JOURNEY through all his trials ultimately have led him to WHO he is today.

Journey Fitness is the true story of a remarkable man who has overcome a tremendous amount of adversity, challenge, and obstacles to not only live his deepest purpose, but to ultimately IMPACT thousands in his community and beyond.

And that man is Travis Barnes.

In so many ways, this book is a story about LOVE. A story about how Travis' eventual wife Cyndy stood by his side in his darkest days, months, and years because she believed in him and LOVED him. And you will undoubtedly find her commitment, dedication, sacrifice, and love to be truly extraordinary and special.

And through it all, TRANSFORMATION.

Transformation of a man. Of a wife. Of a young baby who was born who proved to be so much motivation to Travis.

Over the last few years, I have had the opportunity to work with, mentor, and get to know Travis and I've gotten to learn his story and what makes him tick.

And he truly is one special person. He is now convicted to transform people's minds, bodies, and souls. And he does it as good or better than anyone I know.

I believe Travis' past has forged him to become WHO he is today. A man of faith. A man of conviction. A man of determination. A man of action.

He's a father. A coach. A trainer. A speaker. A businessman. And now an author.

I'm so proud and happy that Travis decided to share his story. While probably not easy to share some of what you are about to read in the following pages, there is no doubt you are going to experience just some of the emotions I felt:

- **Hope**. Hope for the future and all that is to be.
- **Motivated**. Motivated to be a better parent. A better spouse. A better person.
- **Inspired.** Inspired to help more people. Regardless of where YOU are at in life right now, you can always help more people. And that servant-hood attitude to human-kind is wanted and needed.
- **Grateful.** Grateful and blessed for what and WHO is in our lives. Man, we all need a "Cyndy" in our lives to believe in us when the chips are down.
- **WOW.** There were so many times in this book that I just shook my head and said, "WOW." On all levels. And I think you will do the same.

My friend, this book will give you perspective on life. And make you realize that ALL people have a story...regardless of what how good it may seem someone else has it on the "outside."

When I say that "Everyone has a life worth telling a story about...what's your story?"™, I mean it. It is true. Every ONE has a life worth telling a story about. But it's up to you to CHOOSE to do something extraordinary with your life.

And the more adversity and challenge you have faced in the past or that you are facing now, the more people you can ultimately influence and impact. But you MUST be willing to act and overcome...and develop a deep conviction of your life's purpose.

Travis, from the bottom of my heart, thank you for having the courage to overcome. To never give-up. To keep on pressing and believing. And I thank you for sharing your remarkable story. It has not only greatly touched me, I am confident that it is going to motivate, inspire, and IMPACT thousands of other people as well.

It is said that life is a journey and that you must embrace all the steps along the way. And while there are ups and downs, peaks and valleys, good times and bad, we must always remember that with faith, focus, forward-thinking, and follow-through, anything is possible.

Remember, "Everyone has a life worth telling a story about... what's your story?"

Keep the FAITH, dream big, and always, always...create IMPACT!

Much love on life's journey,

Todd Durkin, MA, CSCS
Owner, Fitness Quest 10 & Todd Durkin Enterprises
Lead Training Advisor, Under Armour
Author, The IMPACT Body Plan

DEDICATION

A Word of Thanks

How do I thank all the mentors I've had in my life who have been there along the way to help me learn and help me grow? I'd like to thank my very first inspiration in business, my most recent and everyone in between. I've always been inspired by greatness. My Dad was my first inspiration growing up. He had his own business and I was always impressed to think how cool that was, that he provided a career for himself and so many others all because he had the courage to take a dream in his head and make it a reality. Since my Father's inspiration I have had many mentors who have inspired my career. I want to thank Bill Parisi and Martin Rooney for allowing me into their mentorship. I want to thank Rachel and Alwyn Cosgrove for my time in their coaching group. Thank you to Gray Cook and Lee Burton for the invention of the Functional Movement Screen which has given every trainer a safer, more effective way to program. A special note of thanks for the inspiration and support given to me by author Greg Justice who helped make this book possible. Also thank you Wayne Walker for your time spent editing this book. Last but not least, thank you Todd Durkin. There is no mentor that I have to thank as much as Todd. Todd has been more than a mentor. He has created opportunities for me, been there for Saturday phone calls, loaned me his car, had me into his home, and like a good mentor helped me to change how I think about things. Todd consistently sets the bar and gives me something to aspire to. Thank you Todd.

Next, I would like to thank the women in my life. You will learn in reading this story that my childhood had its challenges but that does not mean that I don't owe my Mother a thank you. Thank you to my mother, Shari Stroud, who is the one who made me believe in me. From the time I was a toddler my mother told me I was special. My Mother's love and special way of telling stories that made me the star helped me to grow up with the idea that I was special and that I could be something someday. Then along came my wife Cyndy, who became the woman in my life that saw something in me when everyone else saw nothing. Cyndy was a heaven sent angel of mercy. Cyndy loved me despite myself and hung on to this toad until he became a prince. Last but certainly not least is my daughter Destiny. Destiny is the best gift that God has ever given me. It was becoming responsible for Destiny and wanting to be a father that she could be proud of that inspired me to become so much more than I ever would have been without her.

Finally I must thank the people that this story is for. I want to dedicate this book to my clients and the members of my TEAM. It is because you share your journeys with me and trust me to help you with your journey that I now share my journey with you. We all face challenges and we all find ourselves in situations by which we are forever changed. It's the journey of life. No one is immune. We all will struggle, sometimes fail, but if we persist long enough, one day will succeed and come out on the other side better for it. If that describes your journey or where you would like to be, then my journey is your journey.

INTRODUCTION

In this book I will tell you about my life, my struggles and my inspirational story of overcoming. You may draw conclusions that I was treated unfairly or that my early childhood circumstance brought about a later adult life struggle. To draw these conclusions would be an injustice. I don't tell this story so that the responsibility for the tragedies of my life should fall on anyone but me. Lao Tzu once wrote, "Watch your thoughts. They become words. Watch your words. They become actions. Watch your actions. They become habits. Watch your habits. They become your character. Watch your character. It becomes your destiny." That is my story. I made choices and that is why Lao Tzu warned us to watch our thoughts and words because it leads to us choosing actions that shape habits which shapes our destiny. The good news is that we can start making better choices at any time, and that is also part of my story. For years I have chosen to hide my story from every new person that I met, because of my fear of rejection and fear of how it could affect my ability to live a successful life. In writing this book, I chose to be vulnerable and risk the rejection of others in the hope that my story could help to inspire people. For too long this secret has had me questioning whether or not I would have the friendships that I enjoy, if those friends knew my story. When a secret is no longer a secret then it loses its power. Thank you in advance for reading my book and taking away the power my secret had over me. If you like this book and feel it will help someone you know then please share it so this story can take on a new power to motivate and inspire.

COMMENTARY BY GREG JUSTICE

W alt Disney once said, "All the adversity I've had in my life, all my troubles and obstacles, have strengthened me... You may not realize it when it happens, but a kick in the teeth may be the best thing in the world for you."

Travis Barnes was "kicked in the teeth" early and often, and tells his story in *Journey Fitness*. This is a book about dysfunctional family relations, drugs, alcohol, and time served in federal prison but ultimately, it's a story of redemption and salvation.

Once I began reading *Journey Fitness*, I couldn't put it down. It's raw, real and riveting. Travis' story begins when he's three years old, dealing with his parents "horrible" divorce and growing up searching for positive male role models because of his mother's poor choices.

After finding his passion, Travis once again encountered adversity through the use of steroids and came to the realization that "The people who I idolized as pictures of health were actually some of the unhealthiest people I would ever meet."

When Travis met Cyndy, his life changed forever. In fact, one of my favorite lines in the book is, "In the end there was one thing stronger than my addiction and that was the love. The love I had for Cyndy was stronger than my addiction." But, if you think we're at the point where they live happily ever after, you've got another think coming, because that's when ADVERSITY strikes again…

It's hard to imagine going to prison as being the best thing in the world for you, especially when your wife is 8 months pregnant, but I truly believe that's the case for Travis, as redemption and salvation were waiting on the other side of the jail house bars.

As a man of faith, I was touched by Travis' journey to God and look forward to the greatness his life has in store.

Greg Justice, MA
Owner, AYC Health & Fitness
Author, Treadside Manner – Confessions of a Serial Personal Trainer

The Journey Begins

was only 3 years old when my Father left my Mother. The only word that comes to my mind to describe my parent's relationship is 'horrible'. Unfortunately for my older brother Erick and me, we didn't have the type of parents that could get along, even as they went through their divorce. We had the type of parents that fought over us, as if we were pieces of raw meat tossed between two hungry tigers. Only thing is, our parents were worse than tigers, because they possessed the ability to speak. Every time we were with one of them, each would spend most of their time telling us how our other parent's behavior was bad and that they didn't love us. I can still here Mom saying, "He loves you just in his own way", which translates to, "He doesn't love you like I do." And our Dad would say, "If she really cared about you she wouldn't be putting you through all of this", and, "Your mother is brainwashing you." This translated to, "You are just a pawn in your mother's agenda to attack me and she doesn't care about you." Visiting my father was never good because he worked all the time and it was obvious that our Step-Mother did not particularly care to have us around. She never did anything fun with us and would frequently tell us to get out of the house and go find a kid in the neighborhood to play with. But, we didn't go on visits to my father's house very often, because our Mom had custody of us and our Dad lived about a two hours drive away.

I was born and raised in the small, rural town of Sayre, Pennsylvania. Growing up without a father around left me searching for other male role models, and unfortunately, when my Mom remarried she chose an alcoholic who spent most of his time in the garage. His name was Charlie. I don't want you to get the wrong idea about Charlie. He was not an abusive drunk. The only thing Charlie did after he drank too much was to fall down and go to sleep. Charlie liked the garage, because he enjoyed being in a place where he could play music, draw, and indulge in other substances. I think that Charlie's good nature, combined with intoxication and his willingness to live in the garage is what allowed his marriage to my Mother to last for so many years. My mother loves to yell. She yells so much that sometimes she yells when she only means to talk. God did not bless her with a normal tone of voice. The point I'm trying to get at is, Charlie was strike two in the dad department for me. This now gave me two absentee dads, one who lived out of town and the other who lived in the garage, mostly in a comatose state. I've learned over the years that boys need positive male role models in their lives. As boys, we need someone to teach us to shave, someone to look up to, someone to teach us how to be men.

I was very young, probably about 6 years old, when I discovered Hulk Hogan, the big blond haired wrestler. I remember seeing his enormous muscles and thinking, "That must be what it is to be a man. I need muscles like him!" I clearly recall body slamming my stuffed animals onto the floor, wearing nothing but my underwear, so I could be like Hulk Hogan. I would do this right in the middle of the wrestling ring, or what everyone else called the living room. This would get Charlie's attention, when he happened to be inside from the garage, and he would occasionally pretend to be Andre the Giant, another wrestler from that era. I forgot to mention, Charlie was a big man. He was 6' 3" and tipped the scales at about 250 pounds. Charlie would always win our bouts, by sticking my feet up to the ceiling until I gave up. Those were good times. I wish they had happened more often.

Unfortunately for us, the game Charlie played more often was go hide and seek. Charlie would take off for days at a time bar hopping, followed by falling asleep wherever he happened to be after he finally had too much to drink. The bartenders liked Charlie (as well as the money he spent in their bar), so when my Mom called around to the bars looking for him, no one would ever admit that Charlie was there. Once she figured this out, instead of calling, my Mom would load us in the car and go find Charlie. I believe this is why I am pretty good at most bar games. As an adult, when I am out in a bar, I perform as well at their bar as some kids do at their sports after having started playing at an early age. Usually once we found Charlie, I would get to play pool, shuffle board or darts, while he and my Mom worked things out.

Still, that wasn't how I wanted to spend my time. I much preferred playing with my action figures, pretending to be the hero. I played with He-Man, Star Wars characters, and of course my favorite, Hulk Hogan. I remember it wasn't long after becoming intrigued with Hulk Hogan that my Mother bought me a Hulk Hogan workout set. I can still hear the tape playing, "Come on all you little Hulkamaniacs! Let's go! Time to get those 24 inch pythons!" I would follow the workout chart and exercise with my little blue plastic covered weights, trying to transform myself and be like Hulk. As I got a little older, Charlie informed me that wrestling was fake. For me, that was like finding out Santa Clause was not real. It wasn't an issue with me whether or not wrestling was real, however it was a devastating blow learning that my role model Hulk Hogan had been deceiving me.

Finding My Passion

A s time marched on, other figures filled the void in my hero department, a void created by disappointment and let-downs by those I previously looked up to. The movie Rocky provided my next inspiration. I realized that Rocky was not real either. I knew Rocky was a movie character played by Sylvester Stallone, but I thought if I could emulate him in life then I would become the ultimate male. I remember memorizing all of his lines from the movie and trying to imitate his voice. My parents bought me boxing gloves and a punching bag, as I wanted to train and do everything like Rocky.

It was around this time my Dad moved back to town, opening a car dealership in our area. He was always so busy that it didn't give us much more time together than before, but my Dad encouraged my interest in weight lifting by purchasing a gym membership for me. I started working out and began reading muscle magazines like 'Flex' and 'Muscle and Fitness', which is where I discovered Arnold Schwarzenegger. Arnold inspired me to read his book, The Encyclopedia of Bodybuilding, which fueled the desire within me to become something more than what I was at the time.

Exercise was therapy for me. It helped me hide pain. I believed my friends would see I had more muscle than they did, and then they would want to be like me or at least want to be my friend because I was one of the bigger guys. What my friends didn't know, is that what I truly wanted were some of the experiences they were having, like playing basketball or a game of catch in the side yard with their Dad. I remember crying at times over the pain I felt watching other boys having those positive experiences. One of my friends was Mike Berrettini, who lived across the street from me. Mike was the same age as me, our birthdays were 2 days apart. I was born on March 15th, the Ides of March, and Mike was born on Saint Patrick's Day, March 17th. Mike's Dad, Lee, owned a local pharmacy and he was always very good to me. On occasion Lee played basketball with both Mike and I in their backyard which helped me feel better about not having my Dad around. It's amazing how God brings people into your life when you need them, with a plan and purpose so much greater than one might realize at the time.

Mike and I stopped going to school together in 7th grade, as I moved to public school and he stayed in private school. Due to the different paths we were on, we eventually became disconnected. I continued to life weights and as time went by, the owner of the gym where I was a member took an interest in me. His name was Andy, and he was the Masters USA bodybuilding champ at the time. With his guidance I began to learn more and more about exercise. I would go to the gym often, sometimes 2 or 3 times a day. I would read everything about bodybuilding that I could get my hands on, and would hang around the veterans just trying to learn anything I could. While many kids were watching a ball game with their dads, I was watching my VHS copy of 'Pumping Iron' starring Arnold Schwarzenegger and Franco Columbo. I learned that Venice, California, was where bodybuilding started and I dreamed of traveling there someday.

I didn't know it at the time, but my brother Erick was envisioning traveling out west as well. Erick was 5 years older than me, and upon graduation from high school he wanted to get as far away from our family as he could. He chose to attend college at the University of Nevada - Las Vegas. We went to visit Erick while he was at college, and I asked if we could stop in at Gold's Gym. I figured if I were lucky, maybe I would get to see some of the people I had read about in 'Muscle and Fitness', and I got my wish. I was elated to see two bodybuilding icons there. One was Shawn Ray and the other was Lee Haney. For those who aren't familiar with Lee Haney, he was the bodybuilder at the time who was predicted to beat (and later did) Arnold Schwarzenegger's record for winning the most Mr. Olympia competitions. Have you ever looked back on events in your life and realized that God was trying to speak to you? Reflecting on my moment with Lee Haney, I see God in action. I vividly remember nervously approaching Lee and asking for his autograph. He obliged, and signed 'Lee Haney Matthew 5: 14-16'. As I walked away I wondered, who is Matthew? Is that the guy he's working out with? And what do those numbers mean? I would later come to learn the numbers are a reference in the Bible, and I believe this was the first time God spoke to me about my fitness journey. Matthew 5: 14-16 says this:

You are the light of the world. A city set on a hill cannot be hidden; nor does anyone light a lamp and put it under a basket, but on the lamp stand, and it gives light to all who are in the house. Let your light shine before men in such a way that they may see your good works, and glorify your Father who is in heaven.

Before I left Gold's Gym, I also met a couple of trainers, Mel and Eric, who were very receptive to me. They took time to talk with me and told me I had potential. I knew after meeting and interacting with them that I wanted to come back to Las Vegas and be like them.

My Mom liked it in Las Vegas too. She had an old boyfriend from high school who worked as a pit boss at the Mirage, and he told her he could get her a job as a chip runner. With my Mother not being fond of the fact that my Father moved back to town, coupled with my brother being in college so far away, she did not need much convincing to move west. I told her I was unhappy with our life in Sayre and that I wanted to move to Las Vegas. So at age 16 and preparing to start my junior year of high school, we sold our house, packed up and moved to Las Vegas. My Mother and I drove across the country, and Charlie flew out so he could bring our cats. At the time, a roundtrip ticket was cheaper than a one way trip, so it made financial sense for Charlie to purchase and fly out with a roundtrip ticket, even though he was not planning on returning back to Sayre.

I had thought that moving to Las Vegas would somehow transport me closer to the things I wanted in life and would fill the hole in my heart that was constantly with me. Honestly though, I had never felt so alone. I didn't have a lot of friends back home, but I did have a few and I had a girl that I had been dating for a few years. (Much later in life, I would learn that I suffered from major co-dependency issues, as a result of feeling abandoned by my Dad.) It was just too much for me to cope with. I had spent most of my life feeling the pain from missing a father, and now I had lost my girlfriend who had helped to fill that void.

I remember seeing the other half of Charlie's round trip plane ticket sticking out of the pocket of a duffle bag. I looked at the return flight reservation date on the ticket, knowing that my mother would never let me leave Las Vegas by myself. I decided that if I was going to go back to Sayre, I would just have to do it on my own. On the date of Charlie's return flight, I borrowed my mother's car to go to the gym. But I didn't go to the gym that night. I called a mutual friend of ours, Denise, and told her I was going home and where my Mom could find her car. Denise tried to persuade me to talk to her, but I just hung up the phone and walked into McCarran International Airport to take my plane ride as Charles Stroud, en route to Newark, New Jersey. This never could have happened after the tragic events of 9-11-01 of course, but I pulled it off even though I didn't know what I was going to do once I landed in Newark. My hope was that as a 16 year-old boy I could choose to live with my Dad and maybe we could have the relationship I had been craving my whole life. I just had to figure out how to get the rest of the way home from Newark, which was about a 4 hour drive if unlike me, you had a car. Thankfully, as events unfolded my parents had arranged for someone to pick me up once I landed in Newark. And, we were able to work out an agreement that allowed me to live with my Dad.

It was a strange situation, living with my Dad. I had almost moved in with him one time before, and even stayed with him for a summer, but this seemed more permanent than ever with my Mom living on the other side of the country. I think it seemed a little too permanent to my Stepmother, who made it crystal clear that she didn't like me being there. Every day was a day of walking on egg shells. My Dad and I had arguments, solely due to tension she created in the home. About a month after moving in with him, my Dad and I had a physical altercation which resulted in a trip to the hospital for me. Because I was still a minor at the time, the hospital staff had to report the incident to proper authorities. A decision was made afterwards that I would move in with my Grandfather. Child Protective Services visited me several times, calling me out of classes at school to follow up and see how I was doing. It was an embarrassing time in my life, going to school displaying the visual evidence of having been beat up and repeatedly being called out of my classes. I never moved back in with my father, but we did reconnect several months later when I began to work for him at his car lot.

I finished my high school years living with my Grandfather who was a kind man that possessed a very positive attitude. My Grandfather liked to cook, watch western movies and drink beer. He would drink about a case of beer every other day. Still, he was good to me. He took great care of me and offered his advice when I needed it. As I settled into staying at my Grandfather's house I began my exercise therapy again. I was the only kid I knew that was working out at 5:00 AM before school. Andy's gym didn't open that early, but he gave me a key because he trusted me. I had found my passion in fitness and I knew I wanted a career in fitness. I asked for and received the American Council on Exercise (ACE) personal training course for my 17th birthday and began to study for my certification.

My First Job in Fitness

The time finally arrived for me to graduate high school. I remember I wrote 'Time Served' on my cap. My school years weren't full of great memories. I didn't like school. When you walk around with something broken inside of you, you don't feel like you fit in. However, my Dad did throw me a graduation party that was out of this world. He gave me a card and written on the inside was "the key is in the pool". I remember jumping into the pool fully clothed, full of excitement and anticipation to discover what that key was for. Was it for a car? If so, what kind of car was it? As it turned out, the key wasn't in the pool. It was in the skimmer for the pool. The pool was just the practical joke component of the gift giving ceremony. Ha Ha. Funny, Dad. The key on the other hand, was not funny at all, as it opened the next chapter of my life. The key went to the amazing gift of a fully furnished apartment. The apartment was pleasantly

equipped with a water bed, black leather couches, and an awesome Pioneer stereo system.

This meant it was time to begin my adult working life in Sayre, Pennsylvania, working with my Dad at his car dealership. It was difficult for me, because even though I had run away from Las Vegas to come back home, the west coast and fitness had never quit calling to me. I just didn't have the heart to tell that to my Dad at the time. I accepted the apartment with a big hug and thank you. After working for him for several months, the day arrived that I finally told him I must leave Sayre and follow my dreams.

So at age 18, I loaded up a rented U-Haul and moved to Las Vegas again, hopeful of landing a job at the Gold's Gym I had visited a couple of years earlier. If that didn't work out, I thought maybe I could find my way to Venice California and live my dream out there. Once I arrived in Las Vegas, I was elated to be able to interview for a position at Gold's Gym. I arrived for the interview wearing my dress clothes and a tie, which really impressed the manager. Upon reviewing my application, he learned that I grew up exposed to, and had some experience with, selling cars. He was especially glad I had some sales experience, and hired me on the spot. My first dream in physical fitness had actually come true. I was ecstatic!

There is a saying that 'having isn't always wanting'. As I began to work in the Gold's Gym, it didn't take me long to realize their primary thrust and focus was on sales. Keep signing up new members and keep the revenue flowing in. I've since learned this seems to be true across the board with all big box gyms that boast having thousands of members. It's impossible for them to know all of their members by name, and they rely on customers paying for memberships they don't use. If they didn't have that type of customer, their gyms wouldn't be profitable enough to stay in business. Once I realized that people I had sold memberships to people who were no longer coming to the gym just a few weeks after joining, I I suggested to my boss that we should call them and find out why. I was surprised, and disappointed, that my idea was not well received. My boss educated me with a new term for members who don't use their memberships: sleeping giants. I was told that we don't wake the sleeping giants. This meant don't call people who are paying for a membership and not using it, because they might respond, "Thanks for reminding me. I would like to cancel my membership". I was learning that I was not working in a very ethical business. I decided that if I ever owned a gym, at my place, we would track people down if they stopped showing up. I thought, and still do, that ensuring customers come to the gym is the first step in helping them achieve their fitness goals. But, I performed my job duties as I was instructed. Part of my job was to pick up lead boxes located at other businesses where people would register to win a free membership. Once I collected the lead boxes from around town, my job was to call everyone that had entered and tell them they won a 2 week membership. This was done to get the registrants into the gym, where we could then try to sell them one of our bigger commitment memberships.

I was not enjoying my job, but I still loved bodybuilding. I was quickly becoming friends with Eric Eckenrode, who was the 1991 North American Champion that I had met a few years earlier during my first trip to Las Vegas. Eric was 5' 5" tall and 220 pounds of pure muscle. Eric's wife Debbie was the 1985 Miss America bodybuilding champion. They were going through a tough time in their marriage and Eric had decided to leave her and he needed a place to stay. I offered him the second bedroom of the two bedroom apartment that I was staying in. I told him he didn't have to pay rent, as I just wanted to learn to be like him. I remember sitting down with Eric one day after he started living with me and asking him if Met Rx was the best supplement for me to take so I could be like him. He told me in so many words to stop being naive and that if I wanted to be like the Romans I was going to have to do what the Romans did. Over the next several months I learned just how unhealthy bodybuilders were. I quickly learned about widespread steroid use, bodybuilders who used cocaine as a diuretic, one guy who smoked marihuana before he trained because he thought it lowered his cortisol levels and let him push his body further, and another who actually smoked cigarettes to control his appetite. My bubble was burst. The people who I idolized as pictures of health were actually some of the unhealthiest people I would ever meet.

My Journey to Addiction

Was this my dream? Is this really what I had been working toward since I was 12 years old? I'm selling gym memberships to people, knowing that most will pay their monthly fee and not use the gym. My boss thought that was the way it was supposed be. I became disenchanted. All of my mentors were drug users and I was becoming one too. One day my boss was treating me very poorly, including threatening my job, telling me I needed to sell more memberships. I thought, "Sell more memberships to who? People who didn't use them? People, who like me, would be let down once they found out that these icons of health were all drug users?" After my boss finished threatening my employment at the gym, something snapped inside of me. I went into my office, and with righteous anger, I grabbed my desk and flipped it over. It was my announcement to the world that my dream had been completely shattered. My boss interpreted my action as a threat and rushed into his office, locking the door behind him. He called the front desk and instructed the receptionist to tell me to leave or he was calling the police. I left the premises, however I left more than a job that day. I left my fitness dream, one that would take me years to rediscover and recreate. I did not become a famous bodybuilder. Instead I had become an unemployed drug user.

At the ripe age of 21, I needed money to pay my rent and ironically, landed a job selling cars. Eric moved out to go live with a woman he knew that worked as a stripper. To help pay my rent, Vinnie, a salesman I worked with, moved into the apartment with me. I quickly learned Vinnie was also a drug user. I no longer objected to drug use. In fact, since I no longer had my exercise therapy, I began drug therapy. I carried a lifetime of hurt coupled now with a shattered dream, so I turned to drugs to numb the pain. My job in car sales didn't last long. I never liked car sales. I always felt like a vulture circling, waiting for the next person to come along that I could sell a car to, which would commit them to years of payments before their car was ever equal in value to what they owed on it.

When I gave up my car sales job, I also decided to give up my apartment. I asked my Mom if I could come and stay with her for a bit. I didn't want to be a drug user. I still wanted to do something that would help others. I put interest cards in with the police and fire departments, hoping maybe those professions were my calling. While I waited for something to materialize, I started working construction. I went out to my first job site and my supervi-sor, Brian, offered me meth. He called it speed and said it helped him get through his long day. There is something about using drugs and wanting to fit in with the people you are around. You know if you refuse to partake in the drug use with them, you never will truly fit in. So I figured why not, since I had tried many other drugs by this point in my young life. After all, it was just speed and I would just do it this one time to show that I was cool. I tried Brian's meth and something happened that had never happened before with any other drug I experimented with.

I became addicted. I would rather have meth than food. I went from weighing 200 pounds to under 160 pounds in less than two months. In no time, my life revolved around meth. I left construction work and became a bartender to be able to party more and make more connections with other drug users. I spent my tip money on meth. I even began to sell meth to help fund my addiction. I made some of my deals at a bar just a few blocks down from the one where I worked. It was called 'The Ginger Jar' and I learned the bartender who worked there was named Cyndy. When I visited The Ginger Jar, I always ordered a diet Pepsi. Cyndy didn't know I was there for a drug deal and she later told me she would wonder who the quiet shy guy was down at the end of the bar with a diet Pepsi. We eventually got to know one another and she learned that I was a bartender as well. After she learned that I worked as a bartender, it seemed that every time I came into The Ginger Jar she had some little job she needed help with. She would ask me to change a CO2 tank for the draft beer system, or lift something for her. I am a little slow figuring out women, but I was starting to get the feeling that she liked me. I remember going into the bar one time just before Halloween and Cyndy told me that everyone was helping to carve a pumpkin, and that I needed to help too. I politely told her "No thanks", but she said that 'no' was not an option. I liked that. I decided to ask her out on a date after that.

My Journey through Hell
with an Angel beside Me

Cyndy was an angel of mercy for me, as I was taking a journey through hell. When Cyndy and I had started dating, I was being evicted from my apartment. I had been using more meth than I was selling, and my paychecks had become dedicated to funding my addiction. Cyndy took me in and let me stay with her. She had learned what I was into, yet she chose not to throw me out, even though I continued to use meth. The only thing she required of me is that I slept and ate once in a while. Cyndy and I were only together for a few short months when I decided to propose to her. I knew I needed her in my life. If not for Cyndy, I'm certain I would have never survived my journey through hell. It's a fact, without her I would not be here today.

I will never forget the day that Cyndy saved my life. I had planned to meet Cyndy and my brother Erick at a bar in Las Vegas called Danny's Slots. I had been up all night partying with Brian, and about 20 minutes before Cyndy and Erick met me at Danny's Slots I took a gel cap with meth in it. It must have been just too much meth for my system to handle. A couple of minutes before they arrived to meet me, my jaw began to chatter so badly that I could barely talk. Cyndy and Erick quickly noticed what was happening to me and helped me to the car. By the time they got me in the car, my body was starting to convulse. They rushed me to the hospital. As I arrived at the hospital emergency room (ER), nurses quickly took over with my care and rushed me into an ER treatment room. They took measurements of my heart rate and blood pressure and I remember hearing one of them yell to the doctor, "We got to get him under control fast before his heart explodes". A different nurse was standing at the head of my bed and I remember asking her, with words I could barely utter, "Am I going to die?" She looked at me and said, "We're going to do what we can". That was not the response I was expecting or hoping for. Several hours later I woke up with all sorts of medical equipment attached to me and saw Brian sleeping next to me in a chair. I asked, "What's going on?" He said, "We are waiting on CAT Scan results to see if you had any brain damage. They said it was like you gave yourself a self-induced stroke".

I am embarrassed and disgusted to admit it, but my addiction did not end there. I was busted once in a parking lot while with a friend who was making a drug deal. It was a frightening event. We had hoods put over our heads, to help protect the identity of the undercover cops that were present. I wondered if they were going to kill us, because I didn't understand the necessity of the hoods at the time. In fact, I even wondered if it was really cops who had arrested us. Another time I was at Brian's house when it was raided by police busting open the door, some carrying military style weapons, and throwing us all down on the floor with their weapons pointed at us. It wasn't only the police who had guns. There were drug deals that went bad. I remember one morning just before

Christmas I was in the hotel room of a Mexican gangster who thought he had been cheated by my associate. I ended up on the wrong end of a gun, staring up the barrel at a Mexican gang-banger with a shaky hand who had been up all night and was contemplating whether he would shoot me or let me go. Luckily for me, he chose to let me go. However, fear of the police or death itself was not stronger than my addiction.

In the end there was one thing stronger than my addiction and that was love. The love I had for Cyndy was stronger than my addiction. Cyndy and I were married along the way, and the arrests I mentioned landed both Brian and I in a drug rehabilitation program along with a probation sentence. I could have been sentenced to prison but I was given another shot at life through probation and the rehabilitation program. I decided it was time for a change. I did not want to lose Cyndy by going to prison. I stopped using drugs and even started attending church. I began working construction again while attending realtor school. I also began praying that God would bless Cyndy and me with a baby. I felt I was ready to be a father now that I was clean and focused on the future.

My Journey to Prison

will never forget the day. I was at a roofing job with Brian, as we were still working together, when he asked me to drive him to pick up pseudoephedrine pills, which are used to manufacture meth. I preached to him about getting clean as I drove him there. He promised this would be the last time. He even offered to take my car himself but instead I drove, afraid to let him down. I was always afraid to let anyone down. I was always willing to harm myself as long as I still had the acceptance and approval of others. We drove into a mini-mart parking lot in my wife's Mustang convertible, where we purchased pseudoephedrine pills from an Arabic man, unaware that Federal Law Enforcement Agents were observing the entire transaction. They watched us fill the trunk of my wife's convertible with boxes of pseudoephedrine pills and then drive away. They followed us, so they could learn where we were taking the pills to, hoping we would lead them to a meth lab. We dropped the pills off at a storage locker that Brian rented, and then I dropped Brian off at his house, unaware that we had been observed throughout our activity.

Later that evening I attended a Narcotics Anonymous (NA) meeting. On my way home I was talking to Cyndy on my cell phone and told her I was going to have to hang up because I had a following of police cars reminiscent of the infamous O.J. Simpson police pursuit. I pulled over and the police asked me to step out of my car and walk around to the front of it. They instructed me to place my hands on the hood of the car as they patted me down and searched my pockets. Then they handcuffed me. An undercover detective appeared and informed me they had a warrant to search my home and storage. I told him that they would not find anything illegal, and that I was clean. He said if that is true, then we will let you go. Good to his word, I was let go that night and was given his business card in case I later decided that I wanted to talk to them about the day's events, or any other illegal activities that I might be aware of. I never did give the detective a call.

Two weeks later, Cyndy and I found out that God had blessed us with a baby. I thought about that close call with the police and was so grateful I was not arrested that night and that I was there to hear the great news that Cyndy and I were going to have a baby. Once I received that news, I realized I was going to have another person to love and to be responsible for, so I severed all ties with everyone I knew that was even remotely connected to drugs. Several months went by and I was working at two jobs. I landed a union construction job away from Brian, and I took a second job at Baby's R Us warehouse so we could take advantage of employee discounts on things that we would need for our baby. Cyndy was 8 months pregnant and we had never been happier together.

Then one night while lying in bed, I received a strange phone call from someone asking me for drugs. I told the anonymous voice on the other end of the line that I didn't do that and to never call me again. I knew it was strange and told Cyndy I had a bad feeling about the phone call. Minutes later there was a knock at the door. It was the police who were there to arrest me for the car ride I gave Brian 8 months earlier, when he purchased the pseudo-ephedrine pills. They had been observing me since that time, hoping they would witness me do something else illegal. The phone call was one last effort to get me for something more. So they finally decided they would arrest me for the ride I gave Brian when he bought the pseudoephedrine pills. It didn't matter in the eyes of the law that the pills belonged to Brian. The pills had traveled in my dominion and control for those 20 minutes across town, so they were mine too. This is a charge that the Feds refer to as 'constructive possession'.

Encounters with God

could not believe this was happening now, after I was finally clean. However I now realize that God had a plan. There is a verse in the Bible that says,

> *As for you, you meant evil against me, but God meant it for good in order to bring about this present result.*

This scripture is from the story of Joseph who spent 13 years in prison as a result of his brother's betrayal, but God used prison to develop Joseph into the person he needed him to be so that Joseph could later save an entire country. God was about to make me the man I was supposed to be. Still God is merciful and He has perfect timing and with Cyndy being 8 months pregnant, this didn't seem to be perfect timing.

When I was arraigned the day after my arrest, I met with my lawyer who explained the charges I was facing. He informed me I was facing 188 months in prison. That is 15 years and 8 months! I could not believe it. I could barely count it. He explained that in the state system I could have received probation for the same crime but Federal prosecution works differently. My lawyer fought for me to be released from jail on house arrest while I awaited a trial, but the prosecuting attorney said that facing such a lengthy sentence made me a flight risk. The judge denied my lawyer's request for house arrest and said I was to be held in custody. My heart was broken. Cyndy was 8 months pregnant and I was to be held in custody. What did that mean? Was I even going to see my daughter born?

I just mentioned that God had a plan and that He is merciful too! It was around midnight later that night as I was lying in the bunk of my jail cell thinking I was not going to be able to see my daughter born, when all of a sudden I hear, "Barnes! Roll up your stuff!" We would later learn the court clerk had checked the wrong box on my arraignment form, as she checked 'house arrest' instead of 'hold in custody', which resulted in my accidental release from jail. Looking back, I prefer to call it divine intervention!

When prisoners get released in Las Vegas, a prison bus drives you into downtown and lets you out. I called Cyndy from the 4 Queens Casino. She was shocked, and of course asked how this could be me calling. I jokingly told her I stole a spoon at lunch and tunneled out, and that I would explain everything when she picked me up. As we talked after she picked me up, we both realized that the jail personnel had made a mistake and they would be coming to get me as soon as they realized it. So we went to a hotel to stay, to give us time to think about the current situation. Cyndy was 8 months pregnant and I was facing over 15 years in prison. Cyndy did not want to raise our daughter without me and I did not want her to either. We talked about running, but in the end, after we talked throughout the night, we knew that life on the run meant we could never take our daughter to her grandparents for visits or holidays, because authorities would look for me there. We also knew that no matter what we did we would always be looking over our shoulder and the police would catch up to us one day. So I made Cyndy promise that she would tell our daughter that I turned myself in because I loved her, and I didn't want her to have to live a life on the run. We went to my lawyer's office the next morning to explain what happened and ask what we should do. He acted swiftly to get me an appearance in front of the judge, to illustrate that I wasn't a flight risk. This action persuaded the judge to grant me our original request for house arrest in lieu of detention in the jail. This provided me the opportunity to see our daughter Destiny be born, as well as to be part of her first year of life, while we did all we could do to fight for my life. Knowing the chance of me not being sentenced to prison was next to none, I started making audio tapes of me singing to my daughter and video tapes of me reading to her. I thought this might comfort her when I was gone, but I would later come to know they just upset her.

My attorney tried everything we could think of to prevent me from being sentenced to prison, and when that didn't play out in my favor, we argued that the sentencing guidelines should be interpreted to give me a maximum of 120 months. But, when the judge's gavel slammed down, I had been sentenced to 188 months in Federal Prison as predicted. In the federal system there is no parole and an inmate is required to serve a minimum of 85% of their sentence. The only hope I had of being home before my daughter was old enough to drive was to appeal the judge's determination.

Only 5% of the tens of thousands of federal inmates get to have an appeal heard, and an even smaller percentage have outcomes that rule in favor of the defendant. We appealed anyway, but I knew I had to come to accept the fact that prison was going to be my home and Cyndy and Destiny, the loves of my life, were going to have to adjust to life without me.

Even considering the time that my sentence could possibly be reduced for good behavior, the federal prison system was going to be my home for the next 13 plus years. I will never forget the in-processing upon my arrival at the North Las Vegas Detention Center, being stripped naked, having prison guards inspect my body to ensure I was not concealing contraband in any of my crevices, and asking me for my wedding ring because jewelry was not allowed in prison. Being a symbol of the love shared with my family, I felt as if I gave them the ring I would be losing an even bigger part of Cyndy and Destiny, so I told them the ring wouldn't come off. They responded that I could either take it off, or they would cut it off. I gave them the ring. Reluctantly. I was issued an orange jump suit along with a pair of Bob Barker brand slippers, and then shown to my cell. Well, escorted to my cell.

For many nights I went without sleep. When I finally did sleep, I dreamt I was home holding my baby girl and would wake up with tears in my eyes, at the realization it was only a dream. I paced my cell so much that I was prescribed medication. In prison they use drugs to control crazy people who don't sleep. I chose to refuse the medication. Staying in a comatose state might have made the time easier but drugs put me in prison and I was finished with drugs. I refused the medications and the nurse told me that I would be in trouble for refusing. I remember thinking how funny that was. I couldn't imagine any more trouble than I was already in.

Prison officials decided that since I refused the medication I would need to see the prison psychologist. I remember being brought to her office. She was a pretty blond woman in her late 50s looking much like how you would imagine a psychologist to look. She asked me about the thoughts that kept me up at night and I explained about my long sentence and how it broke my heart thinking of my family. She asked if I had faith because if I did, I could believe that God may change things and that maybe my sentence would get reduced. I told her that I believed in God but that I didn't know if I could count on him to show up. When I made that statement, she immediately began to ask me about my childhood and why I would describe God as someone who wouldn't show up. She learned about my absentee father and the events he missed. She said that we often misplace the characteristics of our earthly father onto our Heavenly Father. I saw she had a point but it wasn't like I could have a sit down with God to find out how I had been misunderstanding him all these years. Or could I?

Eventually I began to exercise in my cell, and I continued to write letters home to Cyndy and Destiny daily. The book cart would come by every day and I would be asked if I wanted a book. I always refused. I was so distracted with thoughts of the outside world that I couldn't imagine relaxing enough to read a book. I was locked in my cell over 20 hours a day, only being let out briefly to eat, shower and call home. Early on, I gave a lot of my food away. I had a rule that if it didn't taste good or I couldn't recognize it, then I wasn't going to eat it. I learned that the hungrier I got the better things tasted. In prison I eventually learned to eat anything, and to this day I will try anything, knowing that it won't be as bad as some of the things I learned to eat in prison.

I was adjusting. One day, the book cart came by again and instead of refusing, I asked what they had available. The trustee, which is an inmate with a job, told me that they had Louis L'Amour and the Bible. I told him that I would take Louis L'Amour. I think God probably laughed when seeing my choice. He had a plan for me to get to know him, to heal me, change me, and one day lift me up, yet I was choosing Louis L'Amour to read. Nothing stops God's plans, but free will can really slow them down! I finished the Louis L'Amour book and kept thinking about what the psychologist said. The psychologist had planted a seed, and I figured that while I may not be able to have a sit down with God, I could learn more about him if I read the Bible. The next time the book cart came by I requested a Bible.

As I read the Bible, I learned how Jonah ran from God. Jonah did not do what God called him to do and therefore ended up in the belly of a whale to allow him to get his mind right. As I looked around I felt as if I were in the belly of a whale, trying to get my mind right. Jonah had to let go of his prejudices and be willing to go and preach to the people that God was asking him to talk to. I had to let go of my hurt that I had carried my whole life and like Jonah, God was leading me to share my story. I was transferred to a different prison in the North Las Vegas system, where they had a youth program called 'A Life of Crime' which was administered by Ms. Patti Kitchen. In this program, troubled youth are court ordered to attend with their parents so they can hear from Police, Correctional Officers and Inmates where their choices are likely to lead them. Upon arrival at my new location, I submitted my application to speak and was quickly chosen. I had no idea of what I was going to say to these kids.

It was going to be my first time as a public speaker and I was going to have to do it in handcuffs and shackles. I spent time writing, and then changing, what I might say. When the time came for me to speak I was escorted into the court room and sat on a stool next to 3 other inmates with about 100 parents and children staring at me. I violated rule number one of public speaking, by bringing a paper to read from in case I forgot what I envisioned my message to be. I was nearly hyperventilating, as well as silently praying to God to help me through this, as I began to speak. I told the kids about how the people that we think are our friends really are not, and how anyone who asks you to do something to harm yourself is not your friend. It went reasonably well for this first time speaker, standing prominently in hand cuffs in front of his audience. I believe I got through to a few who were in attendance, and I think God knew that He was starting to get through to me.

Because I was now part of the Life of Crime program I had gained the favor of Sergeant Kary Kitchen, who was Ms. Patti Kitchen's husband. It was good to have one of the correctional officers, especially one in power, see some value in you. For the most part, correctional officers seemed to hate inmates. Correctional officers are taught that inmates are liars and manipulators, causing them to be apathetic to our circumstances. This probably helps to prevent rampant corruption, but it certainly doesn't help the living situation for an honest inmate.

I was very dedicated to calling home and writing letters daily. Cyndy was very dedicated writing letters back that would include photos of Destiny and drawings from her. Occasionally I would receive a notice from the mailroom indicating that they kept my photos because my wife sent too many, which could mean she sent 6 photos instead of 5. Other times I would get notice that they kept a drawing because it had sparkles on it. The mailroom seemed to be run by correctional officers who hated inmates. Each time I would fill out a grievance form, which was an inmate complaint, and it would go to the Sergeant. I remember the first time that Sergeant Kary Kitchen came to deliver what the mailroom had kept. He saw I had a letter from Sayre, Pennsylvania and he said, "Sayre, I know where that is" and left it at that. It was against policy for guards to tell inmates anything about where they were from, to avoid potential threats, but I had a feeling he must have some family back there since Sayre had a population of about 10,000 people, and no one ever seemed to know where Sayre was located.

Over the next several months I spoke at the prison on numerous occasions, each time digging a little deeper into myself. I discovered that my older role models were really more like father figures to me, and that I was trying to gain their love and acceptance to make up for the love and acceptance I felt I was missing from my own father. I connected on a deeper level with the kids from broken homes. I realized that God was not only using me to help them, but He was also using them to help me.

Eventually I had to say goodbye to the North Las Vegas Detention Center and move into the federal system. I remember saying goodbye to Sergeant and Ms. Kitchen, and Ms Kitchen said, "Maybe we will see you someday", while she displayed an ominous grin. She said, "Maybe we will have dinner with you at Yanuzzi's." Yanuzzi's is a popular Italian restaurant in the small town where I grew up. I knew that if she knew the name of that restaurant, they must have some connection to my hometown. I was moved into the federal system via Con Air, just like Nicholas Cage in the movie of the same name. Cyndy and I had been planning to move back to my home state before I was arrested, because we thought it would be a better place to raise our daughter. Cyndy traveled back to Sayre with Destiny and began to stay with some of my family while I went through the federal process of being shipped around the country like a lost package. I was flown from North Las Vegas to Oklahoma where I spent a month before being flown to Lewisburg Federal Prison in Pennsylvania, and finally shipped by bus to my final destination in Allenwood, Pennsylvania. I was ecstatic to get to Allenwood, because it meant I would be able to have my first visit with loved ones without the separation of glass. All my visits in Las Vegas occurred while talking on a phone and looking through glass at each other. Finally! I would get to hug my wife and hold my daughter for the first time in almost two years.

Upon arriving at the compound I quickly learned that the fastest way to get word to your family of where you were located was through the chapel. The chaplain was not supposed to let inmates use his phone, but he was compassionate enough to allow me to call Cyndy to tell her where I was at now, and we were able to plan our first visit. When our visit finally took place, I was amazed to see how much Destiny had grown in almost two years. Words cannot begin to describe the explosion of feelings and

emotions generated within me when I finally was able to hug my wife and child,
after not having done so for so long.
Human touch is amazing, especially
when it's been years since anyone has
touched you. We only got one hug hello
and one hug goodbye, but it was more
valuable to me than gold. We all started
our visit as early as we could and stayed
as late as allowed. We talked about

Destiny, Cyndy's struggles without me, our hope for an appeal,
and what my new life was like on the inside. By the end of our
visit we had a plan to see each other twice a week. The Federal
prison had a point system for visitations and an inmate could use
up to 12 points per month. Fridays were 1 point. Saturdays and
Sundays were 2 points. Cyndy, being the devoted wife that she is,
told her work that she could not work on Fridays or Sundays
anymore.

Allenwood was much different than the holding jails that I had
been living at in North Las Vegas. When I arrived in Allenwood
they dressed me like a soldier in a Khaki uniform. I even had a pair
of black military boots to match. I have never been in the military,
but the inmates who had been told me that our living conditions
were very similar. We were housed in a dorm style facility, sleeping
in bunk beds which were always supposed to be neatly made with a
six inch fold. We kept our clothes ironed and shoes shined. Every
inmate had a job and we all were paid a small wage to help us buy
food and toiletries from the commissary. There were educational

opportunities and a recreation area. Having a job, opportunity for education and a spot to workout made the time pass much faster than when I was locked in a cell for 20 hours a day. Being able to see my family and have some structure to my day gave me my first hope that my time incarcerated might actually be manageable.

Journey to Redemption

waited anxiously on word for my appeal. There was a chance to get back almost 6 years of my life and it consumed my thoughts. I didn't know whether I would win or not, but I prayed for a favorable ruling. I made a promise to myself that I was going to return home as the best father and husband that I could be. I had heard there were some jobs on the compound that paid as much as $1 per hour, and with overtime, an inmate could earn a few hundred dollars a month to send home. I began pursuing those jobs and eventually was able to obtain one working in the commissary. While working in that position, I also began working toward a business degree and started studying again for my personal training certification. In my spare time, I provided personal training to other inmates and they paid me with tuna and stamps, which was common prison currency among inmates for hiring out services like laundry or shoe shines.

My busy schedule was a good distraction to keep me from being consumed by thoughts of my pending appeal. We knew that the appeals process could take a year or longer to come to a decision, and that there was a 95% chance that it would be denied once the process had run its course. In prison, inmates are assigned a case manager who assists with formulating a release plan as well as handling receipt of your legal mail. The day finally arrived when I was called to my case manager's office for receipt of legal mail. I had a pit in my stomach. As she was not allowed to open the mail herself, my case manager handed the sealed envelope to me because I was required to open it in her presence. With shaking hands, I removed the letter from the envelope and read that my case had been remanded for resentencing. This meant that the sentencing judge would hear arguments as to why my sentence should have been different, and then he could choose to let the original sentence stand, reduce it, or as occurs in some cases, increase it. It was not reassuring, but it was a chance and I was going to try to trust in God that it was going to turn out well.

It wasn't long before I was back on Con Air flying through San Bernardino, California, to arrive in Las Vegas. That only makes sense if you are in the federal system. San Bernardino was a rough prison where rival gang fights broke out regularly. We were required to walk into the chow hall with our hands folded in front of us and no talking was allowed, or your food would be thrown away. When I finally got to Las Vegas it wasn't much better, but it was familiar and I was looking forward to seeing Sergeant Kary Kitchen and Ms. Kitchen again. It strangely felt like returning home. It's amazing how comfortable you can grow into certain conditions. I began to understand how people with no family support or hope of a future could make a home of being incarcerated.

During my original sentencing process, my family had pooled thousands of dollars together hiring the best attorneys, hoping they would be able to make a difference in the outcome of my case, but now we were broke and I was going to have a court appointed attorney. I had heard horror stories about public defenders and court appointed attorneys and I was understandably nervous. I quickly readjusted to the conditions of North Las Vegas as I waited for my first appointment with my attorney. One day I was lying in my bunk reading a book when the prison guards came to get me from my cell for the first meeting with my court appointed lawyer. They escorted me to the prison's legal meeting room where I met my attorney, who was wearing blue jeans. I thought, "This is not good, he doesn't even *look* like a lawyer." Then we began to talk and he took time to learn more about me in-depth than any of the high priced lawyers we employed in the past. Some of those highly priced lawyers are worse than the worst of car salesman. They take thousands of dollars from you and you never see them again until your day in court, and on that day, you can tell they barely learned your case. At the end of our meeting, my attorney advised me that we needed to postpone the resentencing hearing because there was good to be said about me, and my first sentencing report did not highlight anything good. I didn't like the idea of being away from Allenwood for a longer period of time, because I couldn't see Cyndy and Destiny, but if it gave us a better chance of getting almost 6 years of my life back then it was a sacrifice we had to make.

During my extended stay I was able to reconnect with Sergeant Kitchen and Ms. Kitchen, and I was allowed to once again speak in the youth program. I met with my lawyer a couple of more times before re-sentencing, and during one of our meetings, he shared with me that he attended church with the judge. I remember returning to my cell thinking, "What are the odds that in a city of a half of a million people that I would be appointed a lawyer who went to the same church as my sentencing judge?" I didn't know the odds, but I knew they were very low and I began to wonder if God was intervening again on my behalf. I prayed daily. By this time, I had read the Bible. Twice. I had learned how God helped people like Paul out of prison and I was hoping he would help me too.

When resentencing day arrived, I was so intimidated walking into that courtroom. The last time I saw this judge it appeared to me that he hated me. The judge announced the court case as United States vs Travis Barnes. I always thought that sounded very harsh. It made it seem to me as if the entire country was against me. The judge announced, "I'll hear from the defense first." My lawyer opened and spoke about the sentencing guidelines and indicated what my sentence should have been. He also went on to say there were other factors that should be taken into consideration. He spoke about how I had begun to educate myself and detailed how I had participated in troubled youth programs. After my lawyer finished his argument, he sat down. I swear I could almost see the judge smiling. He then announced, "I'll hear from the prosecution now." The district attorney stood up and argued that everything I had done was just a show for the resentencing and that my sentence should not be reduced. The judge then allowed my family and me to provide testimony on my behalf. My family assured him I was worth saving. They told him that I had just succumbed to an addiction and fallen in with the wrong people. I spoke of my pain and regret for the choices that I had made. I told the judge that what hurt me the most was how this had impacted my family. I told the judge how God had been changing my life and that the true reason behind the positive things I was doing in prison was so that I could one day be a better father and husband when I returned home. After the testimony concluded, the judge decided to take a short recess. I saw him ask his clerk to look something up and I knew that was a sign he was considering making a change to his original decision. Once the judge returned from recess, the bailiff instructed us all to rise and as we did, my knees shook. The judge sat down and the bailiff announced that we could be seated. The judge began, "I have reviewed this case and I believe that it is a ridiculous argument to say that Mr. Barnes did all of his good works in preparation for an appeal that he may never have gotten. Mr. Barnes was sentenced incorrectly, and so for that, I am reducing his sentence to 151 months. Furthermore, I believe that what Mr. Barnes has done for his post sentencing rehabilitation should further mitigate his sentence, and so Mr. Barnes, you are hereby sentenced to 120 months".

I was resentenced to serve 10 years in prison, but I was elated! That was 5 years and 8 months less than when my sentence began. The US Marshalls took me back to my holding cell where other inmates were awaiting their sentencing, and they could see I was happy. They asked how much time I got and when I told them 10 years they could not understand my excitement. Those inmates were there hoping for less than 5 years for bank robbery and illegal possession of a firearm. It didn't matter a bit to me that the other inmates could not understand my excitement. I knew that I had received something to celebrate and to thank God for.

It took almost a year for me to get back to Allenwood due to the legal postponements and the slow transportation through the federal system. It was very difficult to go that long without seeing Cyndy and Destiny. By the time I had a visit again at Allenwood, Destiny was another year older and much bigger. Kids grow up fast and it is heart breaking to watch your child grow up through prison visits. Being cut off from your wife and child is like a form

of amputation. Still we had something to smile about because for the first time we could see a light at the end of the tunnel. People sentenced to 10 years or less could go to federal camps and federal camps would occasionally give furloughs to inmates which meant that they could go home for a couple of days under the condition that they returned to prison. We finally had something that seemed close enough in the future that we could begin to look forward to it. We could finally talk about seeing each other again in the future and being able to do things that families do together, and do things that a husband and wife should be able to do.

I settled into a routine again in Allenwood, exercising, working at a job that allowed me to earn money to send home, educating myself, and providing personal training to other inmates for tunas and stamps. Most weeks, we would use up all of my visiting points. I still wrote letters daily and I got creative in how I would be part of my daughter's life. At Halloween I drew the face for the pumpkin.

At Easter I drew a treasure hunt map. At Christmas, Destiny and I would color a tree together. I often wrote letters to Destiny for her mother to read to her. Sometimes I would color half of a picture and let her color the other half. I even took a parenting course at the facility so we could use the parenting room on visitation days. The parenting room offered toys and videos for the kids. Our favorite video was Aladdin. I would dance and sing with Destiny to the Genie song, "You ain't never had a friend like me". I made friends with other inmates which made it nice not only for me on the inside, but also for my daughter when she would come to visit because these guys would act like uncles in the visiting room, always waving and smiling at her. If these guys truly were my daughter's uncles she would have come from quite a crime family. One guy known as J.J. had robbed about 20 banks, and my closest friend, Steve Mazzolla, was an old mobster. He was the national enforcer for the Genovese family. Steve was twice my age and had taken me under his wing. We worked together, worked out together and ate together. Steve and I were supposed to get out around the same time and he offered me a job working at his medical business. Steve was powerful. He even showed me pictures of him and President Clinton together. I never had any intention of getting together with Steve outside of prison, but he looked out for me and that was meaningful to me. It was because of my connection with Steve that my daughter got to meet a movie star during a visit. Burt Young, who played Paulie in the movie Rocky, had come to visit the Italians, and because Steve had made me an honorary Italian, Burt Young sat across from us and told my daughter how beautiful she was and that she could be a movie star someday.

I did my best to make all that I could of myself from within the walls of prison. I basically thought of prison as my college and my gym. Over the next 4 years I earned a business degree, a psychology degree, two personal trainer certifications, a sports nutrition certification, a Swiss Ball certification and a SPIN certification. With my certifications I was able to help groups of inmates get fit. Allenwood's recreation department had 6 SPIN bikes, where I taught SPIN classes for inmates that signed up, as well as also having some Swiss Balls that allowed me to teach those classes too.

My family seemed proud of my accomplishments. Cyndy even began journaling her daily food consumption for me and sending it with her letters. I would design workouts for Cyndy and give her guidance on what to eat. She lost 50 pounds as a result and I sent her story to Shape magazine to be considered for publishing. When I mailed her story in, I had purposely left myself out of it. I mentioned that she worked with a trainer and nutritionist, but thought if the article detailed that the person who helped her with her fitness success lived in prison and accomplished it through correspondence, then Shape magazine may have considered it a story that their average reader would not connect with. It's amazing what you can do from prison. I was so proud when I heard that Shape magazine had contacted Cyndy to arrange for an interview and photo shoot with her.

The more things I became involved with, the easier my time passed. Holidays and birthdays came and went. Cyndy would always ensure that Destiny had gifts from her Dad. The hardest event for me was Destiny's first father - daughter dance, as we had to have someone else take her. It broke my heart that I couldn't be there with her.

There was a chance that one day I would get the opportunity to attend a drug rehabilitation program and earn a year off of my sentence. This was the only way an inmate earned additional time off of their sentence, and one had to qualify to be selected for the program. It seemed to be common practice that inmates didn't get selected for the program until their sentence was nearing the end, so one never knew if, or when, they were selected until that day came. That day arrived for me, and I was called to my case manager's office and informed that I was being shipped to McKean Camp to attend the drug rehabilitation program. It was strange hearing this news. I felt both happy and sad at the same time. I was happy I would get the opportunity to earn a year off of my sentence, yet sad because I felt as if I were leaving my home. I said goodbye to Steve and J.J., knowing it would be best not to associate with these guys once we were in the outside world.

I began to think of what it might mean to go to the drug program at a camp, and realized that maybe I would finally get my chance at a furlough. Maybe my daughter would not have to go to her next father - daughter dance without me. I became excited for the possibilities, and upon arrival to McKean I saw something that I had never seen during my six years in prison. I saw no fences and I saw inmates driving vehicles around. These inmates were not driving vehicles into town, but they did operate them within the confines of the prison, and under very strict circumstances, they drove other inmates to bus stops when they were being released. Upon making these observations, I thought that my life was about to get a whole lot better. If there is no fence and inmates are driving vehicles, then I must be able to get a furlough. I remember finding my bunk and barely getting unpacked before I started inquiring about furloughs. I was informed that this camp was assigned a new Warden about 5 years ago, and that was when they stopped allowing furloughs. I felt like I had been kicked in the gut, to put it mildly. All of those years my family and I had been talking about how we couldn't wait for me to get to a camp where I could have a furlough, and now I was going to have to call home and tell Cyndy that they don't allow them anymore. It wouldn't be the first time she had to deal with disappointing news.

I broke the news to Cyndy about the lack of furloughs and settled in to finish the rest of my time at McKean camp. I met Domonic Antonucci who seemed to have a little more influence at the camp than most inmates. Domonic was able to line me up with a job in the library, where I kept the books organized and where it would be my job to teach elective classes to inmates. I began to teach Adult Continuing Education classes on nutrition and studying for the ACE personal trainer exam. I also took some correspondence courses on sports injuries and working with special populations. I began the drug rehabilitation program. As inmates learned about my special skills, I soon began my side business once again, personal training for tunas and stamps.

So many things had changed about me in the years that I was in prison. I was the most fit I had ever been in my life. I had educated myself so much that I was now educating others. Even my speaking ability greatly evolved. I applied at McKean Camp and was accepted for a program called 'Choices'. Choices was a program similar to the Life of Crime program in North Las Vegas. The big difference now, because we were minimum security inmates, we could be taken into high schools to speak to youth. I was much more comfortable as a public speaker now. I didn't hyperventilate or use a paper to read from. I even helped other inmates learn to speak better. As I sat in the drug program with other inmates, talking about my experience with illegal drugs, I felt like I was talking about another person, in another life. I had done a lot of soul searching. I knew my issues. I was always in search of a father and it was the wrong father. I had a bad habit of harming myself for the acceptance and approval of others in order to fill the void that existed within me, created from missing the feeling of acceptance and approval from my own Father. I was no longer co-dependent or drug dependent. I was free of the pain of my past because I had learned to let go and forgive. My parents were fallible human beings just like me. My focus was no longer on the past, but on the future.

One day I was sitting in the library when I learned that the administration was changing again and we were getting a new Warden at the camp. My first thought was maybe this one will allow furloughs. It was December, and Destiny's father - daughter dance would be in April. Typically, the Warden was available in the chow hall at lunch time for any questions. I stalked that chow hall for the next few days, waiting for the new Warden to appear, and finally she did. The new Warden was a tall black lady, and when I approached her to find out how she felt about furloughs, her response was that there was entirely too much contraband coming into the camp for her to be able to consider furloughs, and she doesn't plan to change any policies that the last administration had in place. I could tell that this was going to be a challenge, but I was up for it. I believed that God was going to help me take Destiny to a father - daughter dance. I went back to the library and began to type a letter to the Warden detailing all of the extraordinary things

I had accomplished while in prison. I challenged the Warden to think of me as a positive example, and that if she gave me a furlough then maybe other inmates could see the reward in model behavior. I asked her to consider my little girl who was innocent and deserved to have her father take her to the dance. I submitted my letter to her office and awaited a response. I haunted the chow hall, watching for her. I caught her there one day, only to find out that she hadn't had a chance to read her mail yet. I finally was able to speak to her another day in the hallway and asked if she had read my letter. She replied, "Mr. Barnes, if you are going to be the first inmate to have a furlough from this camp in over 5 years, then I am going to need it to be for something more than a dance recital". I tried to explain that it was a father - daughter dance, not a recital. She interrupted me, saying, "Mr. Barnes, don't you have some sick relative that you are worried won't be around when you get out?" I got her message loud and clear. She was considering my request. Both of my grandparents had heart attacks while I was in prison, and I lost my nephew who I was very close with, so it was easy to identify family members with health concerns. I re-submitted my furlough request, this time requesting to visit family members with ill health and it was approved. You can call it a change in administration. I look back on it as another moment of divine intervention. In my mind, God made a way where there was no way. It was as good to me as it must have been for Moses when God parted the sea for him.

The time leading up to the furlough was intense. The Warden did not want me to tell other inmates. She knew I would be a target if I did. Inmates get jealous and if one inmate wanted to get rid of another, then they could plant contraband in their living area. I suspected that some of the guards knew about the approval, because I seemed to have more focus on me than ever. They appeared to be watching for me to make a mistake so I would screw up my furlough, but I was determined not to let my daughter down.

The day came for my furlough. I was instructed to be in the lobby of the prison at 0800 hours and I was to return the next day at 0800 hours. If I were a minute late I would be considered an escaped convict and treated as such with loss of all good time earned, removed from the drug rehabilitation program, and shipped back to a higher security prison. I was not concerned about making it back on time. I was just pacing the floor over the excitement of what it was going to be like to drive off in a car with my wife. They finally opened up the door and told me I could leave. Cyndy was waiting outside and I had never seen her look so beautiful. We embraced, and then kissed, like never before. I truly was lost in her touch.

We drove off on our 3 hour journey home to surprise our daughter. The outside world seemed a little different. Cell phones were smaller. They no longer extended from your ear to your mouth. When the first family member called Cyndy's cell phone to see how I felt being in the free world, I didn't know how to properly use the phone. I would hold the mouthpiece near my mouth and speak, then quickly move the phone up to my ear so I could hear the caller talk. I kept it going back and forth, until Cyndy told me that I didn't have to do that. We stopped at a highway rest stop, where the sinks and toilets were all automatic. I was presented a challenge by the automatic hand

48

soap dispenser. It was an automatic one with a catch tray, which I thought was the pull lever to cause the soap to dispense. In my effort to obtain some soap to wash my hands, I pulled on it, when to my surprise it accidentally broke.

As we drove toward our home, Cyndy told me how depressed Destiny has been about going to the father - daughter dance. We had kept it a surprise that I would be coming home, just in case something happened or the Warden changed her mind about giving me a furlough. Destiny thought she was going with a friend from school and her friend's dad. As we were getting closer to the house, Cyndy and I made a plan to give Destiny the surprise of a lifetime. Cyndy dropped me off out behind the house and I got up on Destiny's trampoline where I laid down, dressed in jeans and a sweatshirt. These were clothes that Destiny had never seen me wear before. I even had a knit cap on, because it was cold outside. Meanwhile, Cyndy called Destiny to tell her that her Dad sent a surprise to her, in honor of the father - daughter dance and it was outback on the trampoline. Destiny approached the trampoline with caution, the phone still pressed to her ear, wondering who the strange man was laying on the trampoline. I stood up and she took a step back in disbelief. Shocked at first, she didn't know what to say or do. Then finally, she hugged me and we began to jump on the trampoline.

The next 24 hours were astounding. After we finished jumping on the trampoline, Destiny wanted to go on a bike ride around the neighborhood. We rode bikes and she knocked on the doors of several friends' houses so she could introduce me. It was important to her to introduce me to her friends, because Destiny attended school with kids who teased her at times, saying, "If you have a Dad, how come we don't ever see him. You probably don't even have a Dad." Kids can be mean at times. Destiny and I played the rest of the day together. Then we went to Destiny's favorite place for dinner, which was the Chinese Food Buffett. After that, it was time to get ready for the dance. I wore a suit and Destiny wore a pretty white dress. Cyndy and my mother arranged for a friend of the family to come pick us up in a nice Sedan, since I no longer had a valid driver's license.

Once we got to the dance, Destiny and I went to the dance floor and spent almost the entire night dancing. We danced so much that the other fathers tried to get me to slow down because they felt I was making them look bad. They didn't understand that I only had tonight to be with my little girl. It's a shame that we don't all go through life believing that we need to make the most of each day. The night was surreal. Destiny certainly proved to her friends that she had a Dad, and that night remains as one of the best in my life.

Destiny was asleep before we even got home. It felt so good to carry my daughter to bed and tuck her in. So many times I longed for these little moments. Destiny's night was over, but mine was just beginning. Cyndy and I had a 10th wedding anniversary only

1 month away, and Cyndy had made plans for us to celebrate early. Cyndy had arranged a hotel room for us, complete with roses, rose petals, and a bottle of wine. That night was magical. We made love holding each other all through the night, whispering of how we had dreamed of this day so many times. We talked about how my sentence was almost over and soon we could be together like this all the time. We never slept. We loved, laughed and as morning came, we cried.

That morning, my Mother, Cyndy and Destiny drove me back to the prison. Turning myself back in was a difficult thing to do. The only comfort was that I had only 3 months left before I would be sent to a halfway house, and the halfway house would allow many more visits like the one we just had. The next 3 months seemed longer than the previous 87. I've heard the saying that a watched pot never boils, and I now know that a watched clock doesn't move either. It had been 7 and a half years since I lived in the real world. I was nervous. Destiny had no memory of me being her father outside of prison. And what about a job? What was I going to do for work? Who was going to hire someone who just spent almost 8 years in prison? The closer it got to the day I would transfer to a halfway house, the more I thought about those things. Halfway houses are the Feds way of making sure that criminals get re-integrated into society. Before you can go home from prison, inmates must go live at a halfway house and find a job. If a job is not secured, then it's back to prison for those remaining six months.

My Journey Home

There are two ways that an inmate can be transported to a halfway house. They either arrange for a ride or are transported by bus. The long awaited day for my release arrived and I had arranged for Cyndy to pick me up. This was the first time I would ever walk out the front door of the prison, never to return. I had begun my sentence as an unhealthy, addicted lost boy in my 20s with a full head of hair, and now I was leaving an educated, healthy, driven man in my 30s with a shaved head. I was nervous and excited for what the world might have to offer. I was nervous about work and nervous about being a family with Cyndy and Destiny again. I was hoping I would fit in with them and be able to adequately provide for them. I'll never forget it, July 17th 2010. I walked out through those prison doors and there was my angel of mercy, Cyndy. Many other inmates who had much shorter sentences did not have their marriages survive, but Cyndy had stayed with me. We had been waiting so long for this moment. I walked up to Cyndy, so focused on her that the rest of the world seemed to stop. When I came near, she said, "Welcome Home!" I replied, "Thanks for waiting." We had a victorious embrace and then headed off to a homecoming celebration that included all of my favorite foods. The party was attended by my parents, grandparents, brother, nieces, some old friends, and of course, my Destiny was there too. The party was short, because we had a time limit on how long we could take to travel to the halfway house and check in.

Checking into the halfway house was like checking into prison all over again. I had to say goodbye to Cyndy at the door, and she could not come back again until visiting day. I asked how long before I could get a furlough home and they said that I could start going home on weekends, after I found a job and received two paychecks. I didn't even get unpacked before I started inquiring as to who was hiring, and where I could find a job. A man with long dark hair by the name of Mark had been released from prison about two weeks earlier, and he told me I could go to Dempsey's Laundry with him the next day and his boss would probably hire me.

I put in my request and was approved for time out to look for work first thing in the morning at Dempsey's Laundry. The morning came, and off I went. Mark was right. They hired me and I started the next day. We did laundry for hotels and hospitals, using large industrial sized washers and dryers. The laundry was hot. I had the owner standing over me most of the time yelling at me to move faster and not to drop any laundry on the floor. When I was earning my degrees and certifications while in prison, I never pictured working in a laundry, but it was a job and having it was going to allow me to get another furlough. I had a job in Scranton, Pennsylvania at a laundry service, and the rules of the halfway house were simple. Get a job in the area of your halfway house and you can get furloughs to visit home. Get a job in your hometown, and you can finish your halfway house time residing at home and just checking in with the halfway house once a week. I was a step ahead on this one. I had sent a friend of ours, Denise, my resume about a month before my release and she had dropped it off for me at ProCare Physical Therapy and Fitness, which is the gym in my hometown that she exercised at.

The halfway house had a shared community phone. It was a payphone mounted to the wall in the hallway. If someone didn't pick up the phone within 3 rings, then it squawked tones similar to a fax machine into the caller's ear. I had called Procare to follow up on the resume that Denise dropped off, and was anxiously awaiting a call back. The phone rang and one of the other residents answered and yelled for me. On the other end of the phone was the manager of ProCare Physical Therapy and Fitness. He said, "Hi, Travis? This is Brian Carochi. I am the general manager for Procare and I have been trying to reach you but I kept getting a fax machine. Is this the best number to reach you at?" I apologized and said that I was going through a transition with moving to the area and that I must have left the fax machine on. I told him I did not have another number for him yet. (It was definitely true, to say I was in a transition and I would not be able to give him a number until I got out of the halfway house because there was a rule against residents having cell phones.) "Anyway", the manager went on to say, "I'd like to have you come in for an interview." We set up a time. I thanked him excitedly, and we hung up.

After all this time I was going to get a second chance at fitness. This meant a second chance to do what I loved for a living. I arrived at the interview early. I wore a tie. They liked my resume. I was interviewed by several people and each person seemed to have

Christian undertones in their conversation. I found that unusual, and also thought it was a sign that God had picked this spot for me to work. They thanked me for coming in, and after several days passed, finally called me to offer me the job.

I once heard it said, "Every great dream will be tested". I was ready to take the next step and move home. I went to the people in charge of the halfway house to let them know I had secured a job in my home area. They told me they thought I lived too far away to be one of the people that was allowed to move home, and that it was going to be too much of a commute with the winter weather coming. They wanted me to tell ProCare that I couldn't take the job. I began to beg for the opportunity to drive an hour and a half each way every day. I told them that I was from an area with limited opportunities for fitness and that I had been working for this chance throughout my entire sentence. They agreed to let me commute but told me if I was ever a minute late, even if my car broke down, then I could no longer work there. I had nothing when I left prison but the clothes on my back, so my grandmother gave me the car that I used to take my driver's test when I was 16 years old. Oddly enough, I had to take another drivers test in it to regain my driver's license. I began to use her car to make my long daily commute. The halfway house received 25% of my gross check and the rest went to pay for gas.

When I started working at ProCare, I was assigned to work a split shift because the busy times in fitness are before and after normal work hours for the clients, so I just told the halfway house that I had long hours. The people at the gym must have thought I loved it there, because I hung around even when I was off the clock. I had no choice but to hang around. There was always a chance that the halfway house would call and if I was not there, then I would be violated and sent back to prison, losing my time off for the drug program. Those were some long days. One of my shifts started with me teaching a group training session at 5 A.M., so I would get up at 2:45 A.M. in Scranton so that I could be at work in time.

Even with the challenges created because of the long commute, ProCare was a good place to work, full of good people. I got along well with everyone. ProCare was mix of physical therapy and fitness. ProCare had a positive culture and working around physical therapists was a great learning experience for me. I enjoyed helping out, whether I was on or off the clock. There were only a couple problems. I worked with two other trainers that had only one client each. They told me it was because no one in the area wanted personal training. I found that hard to believe, because even people in prison wanted personal training. My second problem was that I had a boss that was never there. Many times the owner of ProCare, Mat, would call looking for Brian and I would have to act like he just stepped out so that I didn't get him in trouble. I could see the writing on the wall when it came to Brian, so I decided one day to let Mat know if he ever was looking for another manager, that I would like to be considered. One day Mat called and as always, he was asking to speak to Brian. I had to tell him that Brian was not there. Mat was pretty aware of what Brian was supposed to be working on so he asked, "Travis, isn't Brian supposed to be working with you today on the implementation of our new personal training system?" I said "Yeah, he is. I think something came up." Mat said, "Travis, I want you to know that I am aware of what is going on there. I am going to call you back soon." Not much time had passed before Mat called again and said, "Travis, I want this to be a private call so go take this call in Brian's office." I transferred the call and got back on the line. Mat stated, "Travis, how would you like to have Brian's job as manager of ProCare?" I didn't know what to say. He continued, "Brian is losing his job anyway, and I want to give you a shot." So I asked, "When do I start?" Mat said we would meet at 9:00 A.M. the next morning.

I couldn't believe it. I wasn't even out of the halfway house yet and I was becoming a manager. Mat and I met the next morning as he simultaneously met with Brian to let him go. Mat went over my duties and responsibilities. He gave me a company phone and a nice salary with bonuses. He also told me that he had a personal training system that he had invested in, and that he wanted me to watch all the DVDs and be ready to start implementing it by the end of the month. Mat didn't know that I was not allowed to have a phone. Mat also didn't know that on top of the 12 hour days I spent at ProCare covering my split shifts, I also drove 3 hours a day. I didn't think that telling him any of that was going to improve my position with the company so I kept the phone hidden and I bought a DVD player for the car so I could listen to the DVDs on my commute to and from work. I've learned that sometimes you have to break rules to get what you want, as long as you are not doing anything immoral or unethical.

When I took over managing ProCare, it was a failing business that made most if its revenue from sleeping giants (customers that paid for gym memberships they didn't use). Under my management, ProCare grew from training 5 people to training 200. We started to host Biggest Loser contests that grew our weight loss program and I developed corporate revenue as well. Mat had me constantly listening and reading books on leadership and business. I devoured everything that he gave me. I began to build a talented team of people who believed in ProCare's vision. We learned who the top fitness pros in the industry were and I sought them out so that I could learn from them, absorbing what was useful and implementing it for ProCare. For 17 weeks I commuted 3 hours a day 6 days a week until the day finally came, when I was released from the halfway house.

That day was January 7th, 2011, and a major snow storm was underway. I had prayed many times during my daily commutes that the rough weather would hold off until I was released. After looping my car around on a highway exit ramp, I wished I had prayed for one more day! The roads were horrible and I was supposed to drive 2 hours from Scranton to Williamsport, Pennsylvania, to check in with my probation officer. And then another hour and a half drive from Williamsport to home. Now that my incarceration was over, I could begin the supervised release portion of my sentence.

In addition to my prison sentence, I was mandated to serve 3 years on federal probation supervision. I checked in with Officer Kehler, who was my supervising probation officer, and he already knew a lot about me. Officer Kehler was at Allenwood in the Special Investigations unit while I was there, and he still had pictures of Steve Mazzola and me hanging out together. Officer Kehler told me he was impressed by all of my accomplishments and the work I performed with troubled youth programs, but if I am ever found around Steve Mazzola, I will be sent right back to prison. I had no intentions of keeping felonious company, but I did find it interesting that he was taking pictures of us even while we were in prison. Steve was so high profile, apparently they kept an eye on him and who he associated with even while he was in prison.

My incarceration was over and my supervised release began. I mentored with top fitness professionals Bill Parissi, Martin Rooney, Alwyn Cosgrove, and Rachel Cosgrove. These people had some of the top fitness businesses in the country and had trained some of the best athletes in the world. I wanted to be the best, and I knew for that to happen, I had to learn from the best first. Alwyn and Rachel Cosgrove owned Results Fitness, and according to Men's Health Magazine, it was the number one personal coaching center in the country. Rachel and Alwyn had a mastermind group that I joined. I started making regular trips to their personal coaching center in Santa Clarita, California so I could study them and fashion ProCare to be more like their coaching center. Mat saw all that I was absorbing, and wanted to improve 3 other fitness centers he owned, so I received another promotion to Chief Operations Officer of all four of his fitness centers. During one of my trips to Results Fitness, an opportunity was presented to help co-author a book that Alwyn and Rachel were writing. I jumped at the chance. The book became a number one best seller and we were all featured in USA today. In less than 2 years I went from working in prison, training people for tuna and stamps, to working in a hot and sweaty laundry, to becoming a trainer, to manager, and to C.O.O. of four fitness centers. I felt like Joseph of the Bible who had to be humbled so he could be exalted. Joseph did 13 years in prison and then became second in command next to Pharaoh for all of Egypt.

All of this success made for a good life for Cyndy, Destiny and me. It was a busy life and I wanted to slow down so we could have more time together, but the demands of my job did not allow for that. My job did however, allow me to hire my wife, Cyndy, as a personal trainer. Cyndy worked in a deli at the time, and she was so good with her customers that many frequently brought her gifts as a thank you for her quality customer service. I knew that with her caring spirit, coupled with her inspiring story that had been published in Shape magazine, that she would be a great trainer regardless of whether or not she had any formal training. I've always believed that hiring a relational person with a personality was more important than hiring an educated person. I convinced Mat to let me hire her and she quickly became the most popular trainer on my team with our clients.

One day while working at ProCare, I was in my office when a call came from the front desk that someone was there to see me. I asked who it was because this usually meant that someone who did not have an appointment was there to try to sell me something. Uncharacteristically, the front desk put the person who was requesting me on the phone, and to my delightful surprise the voice on the other end said, "Travis, this is Patti Kitchen. Kary and I wanted to know if you would like to go have dinner at Yanuzzis". I ran out from the back office to hug and say hello to the only people who treated me like a human being while I was incarcerated. They told me they were retired now, and that Kary was from the area and that they spend 6 months of the year there, and 6 months back in Las Vegas. Kary and Patti would become like members of the family to us, having many dinners and even vacationing together.

Cyndy and I both were making a good living, and after 11 years of marriage we were finally able to buy our first house. There are many hidden costs when buying a house, so we celebrated when we found out that we were not in a flood zone and that we did not need flood insurance. The house was a fixer upper and it was going to need some work before we moved in. One rainy night we were working on the house when a fireman knocked at the door and told us we were going to have to evacuate because of a potential flood. We bought our house in  August of 2011 and the following month it was flooded to the second floor. It was days before we could even access our house. Our neighbor had been rescued by boat. We kayaked across the front yard to get our first look at all the damage to our house. It was destroyed. There were broken windows, fish swimming in the basement and the smell of fuel and sewage in the air.

I had dealt with adversity before, and if required to make a choice, I'd rather have a flooded house than a prison cell. As soon as it was permitted, we entered our home and began gutting it from top to bottom. We were blessed with the help of the staff at ProCare and the entire community. One of the corporations I was working with through ProCare even paid their workers to come help us. We had a line of people taking buckets of mud from our basement. We had hammers tearing down sheetrock and flooring being ripped up from every room in the house. By the time we finished removing everything that was destroyed by the flood, you could stand in the basement and see the roof of our two story house. There was nothing left but a frame, no wiring, no HVAC, no insulation, nothing.

Cyndy, Destiny and I moved into a FEMA trailer and went back to work, using our spare time on nights and weekends to fix our house, from pay check to pay check. Several times over the next 16 months of repair work, we were blessed with the help of Christian missionary groups who took vacations from their regular jobs solely for the purpose of coming to help people like us who had been through a natural disaster. It was almost worth the flood to see how God worked through so many people.

Meanwhile at ProCare, things could not have been any better. Mat and I had become very close friends. We went to church together. We went on a ski trip together. Mat and I were so close that some of the other staff members were actually jealous of our relationship, but what could they say. We weren't doing anything wrong and I was certainly not gaining any undeserved favor. All of the gym locations were developing personal training programs that they never had before. The book was getting us a lot of attention. We were asked to do a book signing at the local library and we were asked to speak at the Wynn Hotel in Las Vegas, Nevada, on the integration of Physical Therapy and Fitness for a national convention of physical therapists. Mat had always wanted to write a book and he always wanted to speak at the national convention of physical therapists, so when I wrote our portion of the Results Fitness book, I put Mat's name on it and asked him for his input.

Problems began between Mat and I following our presentation in Las Vegas. Everyone wanted to talk to me about fitness, because I was the one with the knowledge and it was obvious to me that bothered Mat. When we went to the book signing at the library, they had accidentally left Mat's name off of the flier for the event and he tore it down, asking if I made the flier. Mat was starting to get jealous that I was the face of his company, and now those within the company who had ever been jealous of our relationship now had Mat's sympathetic ear. Mat started having talks with me about things that didn't make sense to me. He began to micromanage me on things as trivial as the purchase of a vacuum cleaner. Mat wanted to make sure that I knew he was the owner of the business.

On November 23rd, 2012, just two days after Thanksgiving and while still living in a FEMA trailer, I was fired from my position at ProCare. Mat and I had suffered a strained relationship for several months, but I never thought he would fire me in the manner that he did. Mat simply showed up one morning, walked into my office and handed me a termination letter, then quickly left, leaving a coworker there to help me pack up my things. Cyndy was in the other room teaching a fitness session and heard what was taking place. True to the woman she had always been, Cyndy walked out on ProCare, leaving with me as if I were Tom Cruise in the movie 'Jerry McGuire'. There is never a good time to lose a job, but losing your job during the holidays is especially terrible, and for Cyndy and I both to lose our jobs made it doubly difficult.

Journey Fitness Begins

A s I mentioned earlier, we were from a small town that did not offer many fitness related employment opportunities, and I had an agreement with Mat to not compete against him if I was ever let go. If I desired to continue working in fitness, I was required to work at least 15 miles from ProCare, or wait 2 years from the date I was fired. My employment agreement with Mat stated he could sue me if I deviated from the agreement. I began to contemplate, but only for seconds, if I would look for another line of work. I was very quick to decide that I could not do that without committing spiritual suicide. I knew that God had a plan and purpose for my life, and that it involved fitness. As word got out what had happened at ProCare, many of ProCare's clients began to cancel their memberships. Some of the clients that left ProCare contacted Cyndy and I to inquire if they could train with us. They didn't care where the training took place, and some were even willing to have sessions in their home or our FEMA trailer. As I said earlier, sometimes to accomplish things you have to break a few rules as long as it is not morally or ethically wrong. Cyndy and I opened a new chapter in our lives, as traveling train-ers. I had a Harley motorcycle for my transportation, and Cyndy drove a Nissan Sentra. We used her Sentra to support our road show, the trunk loaded with kettlebells and the rear seat filled with stability balls. We traveled from place to place, trying to still work at what we loved and have enough money to pay the bills. On occasion, we would leave a training session and go straight to pick Destiny up from school, and she would have to ride in the small back seat sandwiched between stability balls. Being traveling trainers wasn't the best circumstance, but on the positive side, we were all spending more time together. However, traveling house to house is not a good way to make a living, and we knew it couldn't go on forever. We were contemplating thoughts of trying to continue work in fitness in our area by opening our own place, as many people told us that a non-compete agreement isn't valid when your employer fires you. Still, this was a tough decision because our former employer had already sent us a threatening letter stating he would enforce his non-compete, and we really didn't have the funding available to fight him if he decided to take us to court.

While I was in prison my father became a very devout Christian. One day he called me on my cell phone and told me he had gone to church and met a woman there named Rosa, and said that she owned a commercial building and wanted to rent it. He said, "I think God wants you to come to Elmira Heights, New York". I argued saying, "If God was going to do anything, he would be helping me figure out how to work in my hometown that I spent almost 10 years trying to get back to, in my hometown where I have already built a fitness reputation". All those years in the car business chasing sales had made my father relentless. He called every day until I finally agreed to at least visit this woman's place in Elmira Heights. I said I would, just so we could put an end to the conversation.

Rosa and her husband, Ray Giammichele, own a salon called 'The Hair Hut Salon'. We met Rosa there on a Sunday after church, and she showed us not only the space she wanted to rent, but she also showed us a 'Curves' fitness center, which was located under the same roof. As we toured the salon and Curves, there was Christian music playing throughout the salon, and almost every wall in the building displayed different quotes from the Bible. Rosa owned both Curves and the Hair Hut Salon, and she was hoping that we would be willing to help her make Curves successful. Cyndy and I had learned far too much about fitness to be interested in working for Curves. In my opinion, Curves employs poor science in their program, and the company was on a major decline as was indicated by Curves locations closing around the nation. The advantage of being equipped with this knowledge about Curves was that we thought if we started our own fitness training that did well in the 1400 square foot area that Rosa had for rent (which adjoined the Curves space) it might eventually provide us room for growth. Rosa was very insistent on us coming there to rent her place. She kept saying it was God's plan and asking when did we want to move in. We told her that we would need to go home and talk about it because we lived 30 minutes away and we didn't have any clients in the Elmira Heights area, so starting a fitness business in this new area is a big decision.

Cyndy and I went home and began talking about starting a business in Elmira Heights. We hadn't been to church since we stopped working for ProCare, but we couldn't deny that this opportunity in Elmira Heights seemed like divine intervention, having a potential landlord that felt God wanted us to rent from them. Although we didn't have a reputation for training in the Elmira area, it was a larger city with more potential clients than the one we would be leaving, not to mention if we tried to work in our hometown we might get sued. We decided that if starting a business in Elmira Heights was truly God appointed, then we couldn't fail. We decided to call Ray and Rosa and request another meeting.

We met for dinner at Guieseppe's in Horseheads, New York. I had prepared a presentation to detail our business plan. Ray was in charge of all their properties and I assumed Ray may desire a few more details about our business plan than Rosa. She said she knew God wanted us there, but maybe Ray wanted to know that we had a viable business plan. I spoke to them about the trend of group personal training, explaining that more and more people were enjoying the benefits of having their personal training provided in a group setting. I explained how people paid less than private personal training but got better results because of the motivation and accountability of the group, a format that ultimately would allow us to help more people and realize more profit. I gave Ray my credentials and told him how I had co-authored a best-selling book and mentored under some of the best fitness professionals in the country. Ray enjoyed fitness and has been a member of area gyms, and he understood that we had a good business plan. He also knew we had limited resources to get started so he offered to let us open without paying any rent or upfront security. This was an unbelievable opportunity, so we shook hands and agreed to rent their space. We told Ray and Rosa we would work hard to secure enough clients in our first 30 days of opening the business to be able to start paying them rent.

We had secured a location but there was still much to do. We needed to name our business, get a business license, obtain a loan for purchase of equipment, and figure out how to pay for advertising for our grand opening. It was intimidating for two people on unemployment to think about achieving the tasks at hand, but it was also exciting to be in the process of creating something special. We decided on the name 'Journey Fitness', because we believe that 'fitness is a journey and not a destination', and we felt it was an amazing journey that brought us to this point in our lives. We wanted to help lead people on a journey that would transform their lives. We chose the phoenix as our symbol because it symbolizes long life, rejuvenation and being knocked down but getting back up again. Like a phoenix, we were determined to rise from the ashes and we wanted to help others that felt knocked down by life to do the same.

This was my chance to do it right, and in order to do it right, I would first have to identify all that was wrong with other fitness program models. So I compiled a list:

1. People paying for memberships that they didn't use. I wanted a place where people would invest in themselves, and not a place where I had to count on my revenue coming from 'sleeping giants' – clients who paid for memberships that they did not use.

2. Lack of personal knowledge of clients. For years I had watched members come through the doors of gyms where the staff did not even know their name. I not only wanted to know each client's name, but any physical limitations

they may have, along with knowing the goal they were working toward at all times.

3. Lack of client assessments. There is a saying, "If you are not assessing then you are guessing". We must assess people before we put them on programs to be sure that it will be safe and effective. We decided we would use a medical history interview and the Functional Movement Screen (FMS) that we learned to use while working in the physical therapy world. This screening measures one's ability to move through the 7 basic movement patterns used in life. The FMS screening is of such quality that it is used to screen players in the NFL and NHL.

4. Lack of help with nutrition. Nutrition is responsible for 80% of our results, yet most fitness places only help you with the exercise portion and don't help you with nutrition education or evaluation.

5. Poor Science. Many gyms are decades behind in their approach to fitness, still instructing people to sit down on machines rather than become functionally fit by moving in ways that they move in real life. We were determined to offer the latest advancements and to always stay educated on the latest science.

It was through this thought process, knowing what was wrong with fitness, that we discovered our 'why' for being in business. Our mission statement and core values were now born.

JOURNEY FITNESS
It's Time To Get Metabolically Disturbed

Life Transforming Personal Training.

We will go to any length to get our clients the results they seek. We know everyone on a first name basis because our clients are like family to us. We will find answers to their disappointments and celebrate their victories. We will know the goal they are working on at all times. If they are in the hospital we will visit. If they stop showing up then we will find them to try to bring them back in. This is called a fitness emergency. Each month we will create fitness challenges so our clients have the opportunity to see what they are now capable of outside of the gym. We will teach our client's the value of the food they ingest. Each week we will arm our client's with new information so they can make wise decisions concerning their health. We will be the guide that took our clients on a fitness journey that morphed their lives from the disappointment that it was to the enjoyment that they dreamed it could be!

JOURNEY FITNESS

Core Values

HONESTY - If we can't get you results or you are not willing to follow our program then we don't want to be paid for what we can't deliver so there will never be a client who continues to pay for what they don't use. On our team passive aggressive behavior is not allowed. We believe in honest feedback and assertive communication.

EXCELLENCE - Striving to be the best. Mindset and habit of exceeding expectations. Striving to create a Disney fun like experience. Our team is required to remain teachable so that we can always learn, always improve and always deliver the safest, most effective program for our clients.

ATTITUDE - Maintaining a positive attitude and work environment Our clients count on us for positive encouragement and motivation which begins with the attitude we display throughout our work day. At Journey Fitness there are no bad days. Only good days and great days.

TEAM - We are one team. No member is greater than the whole and every member of the team must do their part to lift one another up. As the saying goes there is no "I" in TEAM.

"IF YOU CAN'T STAND THE **HEAT** GET OUT OF THE KITCHEN"

We located a loan company that would give a high interest loan to us to buy equipment, even though we were on unemployment. We met with the local newspaper and they agreed to wait 30 days to be paid for our grand opening ads. We did all the painting and equipment installation ourselves. We could not afford a big sign yet so we hung a 24 x 36 inch poster that displayed our logo and read 'Journey Fitness' over the front door. We wanted to be able to focus on the training aspect of our business and not the client billing, so we hired a billing company to handle that task. We had learned the value of partnering with a pain specialist for the occasions when our clients experienced pain that was outside our scope of practice, and lucky for us, my brother who is a chiropractor was also looking to start his own business. He agreed to open his practice in the same building as Journey Fitness and call it Journey Chiropractic.

Everything was coming together. We had just one thing left to do, which was establish our nutrition program. In a previous chapter, I wrote of Lee Berrettini and mentioned, "It's amazing how God brings people into your life when you need them and for a plan and purpose that is so much greater than you realize at the time". Lee was the pharmacy owner that played basketball with me when I was a kid. While working at ProCare I had heard extraordinary things about what Lee Berrettini was doing to help people with weight loss. Lee had developed a diet over the course of 10 years with the help of doctors. This diet not only caused people to lose weight, but this diet also reduced and / or eliminated the need for medications such as blood pressure, cholesterol, and diabetic medications. This diet was reported to be a diet that got people out of metabolic syndrome. It was said that this diet was an anti-cancer, anti-inflammatory, and anti-aging diet. Lee was helping thousands of people with this diet and he was booked for consultations 6 months in advance. I knew that I needed to visit Lee and speak to him about using his nutritional program to help my clients. I wanted everything that we did to be scientifically based and medically backed. I went to Lee's pharmacy and he was as kind as ever to me, taking time out of his busy day to meet and talk with me. We joked about playing a game of basketball. In the end, he gave me permission to print his diet with our food journal.

With everything in place, we opened for business on March 28th, 2013, kicking off our grand opening with a metabolism make-over seminar, explaining our nutrition and fitness philosophies and offering people the opportunity to participate in our 'The Journey Fitness Version of the Biggest Loser Contest', with clients competing to win a lifetime membership at Journey Fitness. That day we signed up our first 14 clients and began our business with barely enough revenue to pay our rent. It was scary, but we had faith in God and the merits of our business model, knowing that our business would grow.

In the early days of Journey Fitness, Cyndy and I filled every role in our organizational structure. Cyndy did the office work and accounting. I handled the managing, marketing, program design, and nutritional education PowerPoint presentation development. We both did the training, client's food journal reviews, and cleaning duties. As our business grew so did our team. Our business became a story of our lives touching the lives of others through fitness and helping them on their own unique individual journey.

THE STORY OF SHARI PASQUALE – MY FIRST CLIENT AFTER PRISON AND LATER A CLIENT OF JOURNEY FITNESS

Like a lot of stay at home moms, I had put on about 30 pounds after having my two children. I was living in Athens, Pa where my husband and I had recently moved and this was 4 hours away from my friends and family. I was not only overweight but was feeling sluggish and very depressed. I was embarrassed to be seen this way. Nothing in my closet fit anymore!

I wanted to feel better about myself and lose the unwanted 30 pounds, so I decided to join the local gym a few minutes from my house. When I went to the gym to sign up the staff were very helpful, they took my measurements along with my weight and walked me through a program they said best suited my weight loss needs. The program consisted of me working on the different gym equipment they had and for me to write my progress in my folder. I can honestly say that I enjoyed this for about a week, then I was quickly getting bored and not wanting to continue.

At this time I hadn't formally met Travis, but I think he quickly picked up on my unhappiness. He approached me and explained that he was a Personal Trainer, and explained what his program involved and the many different workouts that would go a long with it, as well as food journals, and nutrition ideas.

I thought it was very nice of this trainer to take the time and talk to me, but there was no way in hell, I was going to train one on one with this guy, did he not see that I was 30 pounds overweight, and did not want to be doing jumping jacks in front of anyone let alone with this fit muscular male trainer!

Well Travis soon proved me wrong, he made me feel very comfortable and he was always encouraging me to push my limits and to step outside the box. I now looked forward to going to the gym, Travis was always there to greet me with a smile and encouraging words. I felt he was genuinely eager to help me accomplish my goals.

Within a few months of working out with Travis we came to know each other pretty well and I think he thought I found it odd that he commuted an hour and a half each day from Scranton just for a job in fitness so he came to me and asked if I had some time because he would like to speak to me and tell me about his Journey and what brought him to work at Pro Care Physical.

Travis had told me that it was important to him to confide in me and to be honest especially since some of my questions were leading him to either having to lie or to have this conversation. Travis then explained to me that he had spent 8 years in prison, and had recently come back to Athens to live with his wife (Cyndy) and his pride and joy, his beautiful daughter Destiny.

I was touched that he had told me this information, I know it was very hard for him to do, but not once did it change my mind about training with him, it only made me admire his motivation and his desire to change even more. I went home and talked it over with my husband, and told him about Travis's past. Without even really knowing Travis at that point my husband also felt the same way I did. We both felt that everyone makes mistakes in life and if he had already paid his debt to society and was released then we should accept that and help support his journey to build an honest and productive life. We are strong believers in second chances and watching Travis succeed in his personal and professional endeavors over the last few years validated our faith in him and the potential we felt he had.

As time went on I had the pleasure of getting to know Travis' wife Cyndy, who was also a Personal Trainer. We quickly became friends, it's hard not to …for anyone who knows Cyndy she always has the biggest smile for everyone who walks through the gym door, and always knew everyone by name. After about a year and a half of training with Travis he came to me and told me that he had some exciting news to share with me, he was offered the position of Chief Operations Officer at the gym! I was incredibly happy for him, but also very sad at the same time. Travis told me that he would no longer be training me, he did however tell me that his door would always be open if I needed, and that he would always be around checking in to see if I was handing in my Journal.

At this time, Cyndy became my personal trainer and we instantly hit it off! I didn't even feel like I was working out sometimes, she always knew how to make our time together productive as well as a lot of fun! She was amazing, and gave it her all to see that I was reaching my goals every week.

I was loving being at the gym so much, that I would always go home and brag to my husband (Tony) about how many push-ups I did or what crazy finisher Cyndy had me do that day at the end of my workout. My husband could see the difference in me very quickly, not only was I losing the weight but I was also starting to see muscle and I was feeling more confident and much happier with myself, and I could wear my pre baby clothes again!

Travis, Cyndy, Tony and I all became friends at this time. We enjoyed doing many of the same things and enjoyed spending quality time with each other's family.

Travis was no longer training, but was determined to help Tony reach some of his personal goals. Tony again, like many Father's had a very hard time finding time to go to the gym to workout, so Travis came up with a solution... he and Tony would get up at 5am to workout and run, Tony was not too excited about this idea but soon came to look forward to it. This didn't surprise me at all that Travis was willing to do this for Tony. This is just the type of guy that Travis is. He would do this with Tony to make sure he was reaching his goals, and then he would go in to work at Pro Care Physical and work sometimes a 15 hour day! You cannot find many guys like Travis Barnes!

Our friendships became much stronger, and we found ourselves helping each other in many ways, it was a huge devastation that we all went through, On September 08, 2011, when Athens was flooded. Travis and Cyndy had lost their home completely. But these two never quit, from working 15 hour days at the gym to re building their home, these two are truly remarkable people.

When Travis and Cyndy came to us and told us they were going to open Journey Fitness, we couldn't have been happier for them. This is something we watched them both work hard at to get, and we knew we would be right beside  them every step of the way to help them achieve and accomplish their goal, just as they did for us!

Tony and I are both so grateful for having both of them as our trainers, and we are privileged to not only call them our friends, but feel we are all family.

THE STORY OF NEVA KELLY –
RETIRED SCHOOL TEACHER

I have been a member of Journey Fitness since two weeks after they opened.

Travis and Cyndy are "Living Their Dream", and absolutely cannot hide their passion for personal fitness coaching and helping their clients to reach their fitness goals. Their enthusiasm is both contagious and inspiring, and it spills over into every workout session at Journey Fitness. Every Journey Fitness member is greeted by name when they arrive, and the room is full of smiles from start to finish as the workout proceeds. Whether you are a teenager or a senior citizen, Journey Fitness recognizes and evaluates your physical abilities and designs a program that is appropriate for your needs. When I look to my right and to my  left, I see everyone doing what he/she is capable of doing, modified for them, personally. Journey Fitness trainers spend every session giving one-on-one assistance and recommendations to all in attendance, encouraging everyone to make the most of their workout time. Every week is a new workout, and when anyone walks through the Journey Fitness doors they can expect humor, fun music, encouraging camaraderie and an energy level that is through the roof. How can anyone make working so hard be so much fun? Ask the trainers at Journey Fitness

To further build relationships with their clients outside of the gym, weekend "Fitness Challenges" are offered, such as kayaking, snowshoeing, hiking a gorge or even running a 5K. No pressure...if you are interested in participating

great, and if you are not interested, that is fine too. A monthly newsletter celebrates individual client successes as members work toward their goals, there is a forum for recipe sharing and tips for success, and lists upcoming fitness opportunities in the area. Accountability is a great motivator, as clients fill out a weekly Food Journal, get personalized feedback on menu opportunities and learn how they did at the weekly nutrition sessions. The topics for these nutrition sessions are suggested by clients, further enhancing trainer/client relationships.

For me personally, I joined Journey Fitness because of debilitating knee pain, and weight loss was not even on my radar screen. But I now have lost over 42 pounds, have greatly improved knee function with much less pain, improved balance, have less reliance on medications, more flexibility, and all around less physical limitations. I feel that Journey Fitness has given me my life back. We are fortunate, indeed, to have Journey Fitness Coaching, in our region.

COACH JEREMY PURIFOY'S STORY

My name is Jeremy Purifoy and my love for fitness began when I was in high school. I started lifting weights in 9th grade in preparation for the upcoming football season. I always knew if I wasn't going to advance in football, then I wanted to help people achieve their goals whether it was in sports, fitness goals or weight loss. I've always wanted to give the next person the extra motivation and support that I fell short of receiving. I heard about this incredible fitness place that was in my hometown. I knew a few people that were attending and I was seeing great success being attained by these individuals. It was around November 2013 when I first contacted Travis because I heard that they were looking for someone with a passion for fitness, however, at that time I was a little too late contacting him, as the position had been filled. I asked Travis to keep me in mind for future hiring's. In May 2014, I received an email from Travis asking if I was still interested in an internship that could lead to a full-time position. From this moment on, Journey Fitness has been the greatest opportunity in my life. I could not express my gratitude enough to Travis and Cyndy Barnes, because they made my dreams come true in helping change people's lives for the better. I feel that I am rewarded with two pay checks, one that pays my bills and the other is seeing our clients accomplish their goals and having success in fitness! As Journey Fitness grows and expands I want to be involved in every step of the process, and do whatever I can to help Journey Fitness rise to the top! Thank you Travis and Cyndy, for this remarkable experience!

COACH JESSE KING'S STORY

As a kid I was always playing sports. Every season of the year I was signed up for something. Being active was fun and enjoyable. I thought football was my passion. I was a captain on my high school's varsity football team, and I had no doubt in my mind I was going to play another four years in college. However, a knee injury crushed my ambition to pursue an athletic career. Thank God for fitness. I worked out in high school, but it wasn't until I explored more into health and fitness that my perspective, not only on fitness but life as well, was broadened. This knowledge helped open my eyes and heart to the significance of life-long fitness and the impact I could have on others. I began to feel more empowered by my potential to positively impact people's lives. My love for sports and exercise, coupled with the desire to help people, gave my life purpose. I wanted to share the gift of health and fitness with others. The same hunger, passion, and dedication that I had put into football was then directed toward my aspiration to be a health and fitness professional. My mind was made up. I majored in Exercise Physiology in college, and through hard work and dedication, I received my four year degree. However, it was only one milestone. It took even more discipline to buckle down and get my certification. While working odd jobs to get by, and struggling to find time to study for my certification test, doubt started to creep into my mind. It was my faith that I was on the right path that got me through. I earned my certification as a strength and conditioning specialist from a top notch organization, the National Strength and Conditioning Association. Still though, doubt continued to linger. I couldn't find a job.

I don't believe it was by coincidence that Journey Fitness crossed my path. My wonderful girlfriend, Natalina, who has been encouraging and very supportive of my dream to be a health and fitness professional from day one, was willing to explore every option we could find to help me find a job in health and fitness. Both of us were eager to find career jobs. We started making plans to move to Gainesville, Florida, in hope of finding jobs. So maybe it was through divine intervention that one of my best friends, who had been recently hired at Journey Fitness, called to tell me, "Jess, I can get you an interview over at Journey Fitness". Natalina and I were ready to make changes and start our lives, but when fate calls, you answer.

When Jeremy was hired at Journey Fitness, I was extremely happy for him. More than ever, it made me want to get my foot in the door somewhere to start in a health and fitness career. I owe it to Jeremy for helping me get that foot in. Jeremy and I grew up together and share a passion for health and fitness. We go way back. So when an opportunity to work together presented itself, in a fitness career none the less, it was a dream come true. We both always wanted to make a career out of fitness.

On my way to the interview I experienced a mix of emotions. The doubt that I was having about if I was ever going to find a job in fitness was fading away. When I first walked into Journey

Fitness, I thought, "Whoa!" I was instantly blown away by the positive vibes Journey Fitness had to offer. Smiling faces on the clients, a clean and organized facility, and an undeniable sense of welcome. Upon walking into the facility, I only got a surface view of what Journey Fitness was about.

When I first met Travis I thought, "Nice haircut" only because we both have bald heads. Ironically enough, within five minutes of meeting each other, he paid me the compliment of, "I like your haircut". We instantly clicked. I consider Travis to be my mentor. What I learned through my education I consider valuable, but the gems of knowledge Travis has shared with me about being a true fitness professional are priceless. I plan to share these same gems with future trainers, when I open the third Journey Fitness location. I will forever be grateful to Travis and Cyndy Barnes for making me a part of their team. I take it as a huge compliment that they considered me for a leadership role in their company. All I can think is that it was meant to be. We share a common goal; delivering life transforming personal training. Travis and Cyndy have covered every angle to make that goal possible. First and foremost, they treat everyone that walks in the door like family. Client focus is always on their minds. They are very inspiring individuals. Always striving to be the best at whatever they do, I consider them an ideal model of leading by example. I'm very blessed and fortunate to start my fitness career here at Journey Fitness under their guidance.

Today I have no doubt in my mind that I got into the right place, at the right time. I wouldn't consider this to be a coincidence at all. Journey Fitness is not your typical gym, it is a fitness family. I'm proud to be part of the family. As Journey Fitness grows and touches more people, I'll always keep in mind, "life is a journey, not a destination".

COACH MICHELE KELLEY'S STORY

My love of fitness started as a child. I played girls' softball for many years. I played in high school. I was also a cheerleader. Being fit was always a priority. As an adult, I played co-ed softball with my husband Jim. I worked out in all of the local gyms at one time or another. I have friends who would join and soon quit. I was always going alone, doing the same routine over and over again.

I had a couple of friends who joined Journey Fitness. At first I thought "I'll never pay that much for a gym". Well, I was wrong. It wasn't a gym and I needed to work out so I had to give it a try no matter the cost.

I soon learned that it was worth every penny. Cyndy & Travis Barnes are one of a kind. I was eager to get started. They welcomed me, as they do everyone, with open arms. Everyone is like family to them. My first work out was the pumpkin workout. Pumpkins were used all during the workout as a way to make it more fun. Talk about getting "metabolically disturbed"! I had to pull my car over on the way home because I was feeling queasy. That never happened in the gym. This, for sure, was a different kind of workout. This feeling didn't last long. My body soon got used to the intense, but fun workouts. Every week the workout changes. My body was always getting a new surprise. I didn't need to lose a lot of weight but I soon began to. I was eating healthier, gaining muscle, feeling happier, and more positive than ever. I couldn't wait to get to my next workout. That never happened in the gym.

One day, I approached Travis with a suggestion for a nutrition topic. He liked my idea. I said "well maybe someday, I can wear one of those red shirts". I was invited to a staff meeting and soon began working with the team at Journey Fitness.

I have learned so much from the staff and am eager to learn more. I am currently studying to get certified as a personal trainer. I am dedicated to Journey Fitness. I plan to retire from my teaching job in 2 years. At that time I would like to join the Journey Fitness team as a full time employee.

I believe in Journey Fitness. As a Coach, I get great satisfaction from seeing the positive results of our clients. It is so thrilling to see heavier clients who couldn't get on the floor and now they can. I get so excited when a client will push themselves on their BEST SET. This may mean trying the assisted pull-ups, planks on the floor, or running around the building instead of walking. Journey Fitness makes it possible for everyone to succeed at their own pace. I have been passionate about my teaching job for 30 years. I can honestly say that I now have a new passion that I can take on into my retirement years. Journey Fitness is changing lives one step at a time. Thank you for making a difference in my fitness life and in my personal life as well.

ADMINISTRATIVE COORDINATOR DELLA WALKER'S STORY

I was frustrated each morning when I was getting ready for work. I had a very extensive wardrobe of beautiful clothes and nothing fit. I was forced to either buy more clothes or do something about it. I chose the latter, and convinced Wayne to do the same! I came to Journey Fitness in July of 2013 along with my husband Wayne in search of help losing the 50 pounds of weight which crept up on me and the 80 pounds of weight my husband had gained over the years. What I found when I entered through the doors of Journey Fitness truly impressed and inspired me. I met both Travis and Cyndy Barnes, the owners of Journey Fitness. They welcomed us, explained their fitness philosophy and their nutrition program. They showed us client posters on the "wall of fame" which highlights those who have already had weight loss success with them. They listened to our concerns and assured us they could help us tackle this battle of weight loss. I had also set a goal for myself to be able to run again. We left Travis and Cyndy that day knowing we had just made the best decision for our health that we could have possibly made.

The following day, we returned to Journey Fitness to participate in one of the most challenging and fun workouts we had ever experienced. Travis and Cyndy made me feel very confident in myself and encouraged me through my first workout. It was great! Shortly after my start, I began to have some health issues that I thought for sure would side line my training ability. I spoke to Travis on the phone and he encouraged me not to give up. He was willing to provide modifications to my program so I could continue to work toward achieving my goals. He was determined to help me and I was not ready to give up! I persevered and worked through my pain.

Two months into our training, Journey Fitness was having one of their many Fitness Challenges, the Holiday Hold-em. It was a "partner challenge" to lose the greatest percentage of body weight from September to December. The prize was $500 awarded just in time for Christmas. Since my husband and I were just about to embark on a 2 week vacation and I knew I didn't want to be restricted for the Thanksgiving holiday, I didn't want to join the challenge. During one of my weekly weigh-ins Travis encouraged me to give it a try, he had told me he really thought we could do this and possibly win it if we challenged ourselves. I reluctantly gave in and my husband and I joined the challenge. Game on! Now I had to do this, not only for myself but also for my husband. Not to mention, now we had all of our Journey Fitness family and trainers behind us, watching our progress. We did it! We won the challenge! What a sense of accomplishment! We would have never taken on this challenge if it weren't for the motivation, and encouragement we received from Travis and Cyndy's team at Journey Fitness. We accomplished not only this challenge, but also the challenge we entered when we first met Travis and Cyndy. Both my husband and I have lost the combined 130lbs we set out to lose and I am now able to run 3 miles several days a week. We have joined the "wall of fame" at Journey Fitness!

Our story does not end there....My husband and I believe in the Journey Fitness philosophy so much we have both joined the team. I joined Journey Fitness as the Administrative Coordinator in December 2013 and my husband joined as a trainer in July 2014. We enjoy working each day to ensure many others are successful in their weight loss efforts. We continue to welcome clients into the Journey Fitness Family, encourage them through their journey and are supporting Journey Fitness as they grow new locations.

COACH WAYNE WALKER'S STORY

I am 52 years old and have struggled most of my adult life with maintaining a healthy weight. Some of the tools I used to aid my weight control over the years included gym memberships,

racquetball, weight lifting, aerobic exercise, dry saunas, ski machines, Tae Bo tapes, stair stepper, martial arts, ran a marathon, treadmills, Bo Flex, Body for Life, and an elliptical machine, just to name a few. I tried several diets, which were never sustained for a significant period of time. I never found that one component which would allow me to control my weight.

Over the last few years I became embarrassed by my appearance and could start to feel the negative effects of carrying so much weight around. I became winded easily, my clothes didn't fit, and I experienced aches and pains on a regular basis which I attributed to my excess weight. I also became concerned about the potential for accelerated health problems as I age.

In July of 2013, I came to Journey Fitness along with my wife Della, to support her efforts at becoming more fit. I must admit, at first I was very skeptical this new endeavor would benefit me, because decades of other attempts at proper fitness all fell flat.

However, it did not take me long to realize that Travis Barnes was cut from a different cloth. He immediately connected with me on a personal level, greeting me by name the first day I walked through the door to attend a group training session. I was very surprised (and pleased!) to quickly learn that Journey Fitness truly cares about their clients and their success, and routinely demonstrates their ability to make me feel as if I have a private trainer at my side during group training sessions. The trainers at Journey Fitness keep a watchful eye on my technique and posture while performing an exercise, despite being in a group setting. I know the trainers are watching and that they care because they routinely offer encouraging guidance anytime I perform an exercise with improper posture or form. Because I know they are watching and that they care, it motivates me to push myself harder than I ever would have in the past. The Journey Fitness team has a great sense of humor and abounding energy to get me (and countless other clients) excited about being fit. They routinely recognize a client's achievements with public praise and various awards. They engage the community through activities and charitable events tied into our fitness program and goals. The training approach Journey Fitness utilizes is unique and has become addicting. The ever changing exercise sessions remain FUN, and never become boring. It is like attending gym class in elementary school, when you didn't know what you'd be doing but knew it would be fun!

Just as important as the encouragement and motivation instilled by Journey Fitness during exercise sessions is how they have educated and coached me in nutritional matters that contribute to success, and then hold me accountable by requiring me to document my food intake and submit it for review on a weekly basis. Also they weigh me weekly, and no matter which trainer weighs me, they get excited every time they see success on my part. There is an atmosphere of teamwork, and it has inspired me to not let the team down. I have remained diligent in applying the knowledge Journey Fitness has shared with me through their instruction. As I exercise at home on weekends, motivational utterances ring in my head (such as "If it doesn't challenge you, it won't change you") and I push myself a little harder.

I have learned there is no one 'magic bullet' to control my weight, however the multi-faceted approach expertly provided by Journey Fitness has taught me how to be successful, helping me attain a weight that I haven't seen in nearly 25 years! The aches and pains are gone, I have greatly improved physical stamina, and possess the knowledge of how to eat properly and exercise in order to maintain the success Journey Fitness has helped me achieve. If anyone would have told me in July of 2013 that I would lose 80 pounds by mid-December of that year, I would have laughed at them. However, the staff at Journey Fitness knew it was possible and provided me the motivation and tools to make it happen. Instead of feeling like I am aging rapidly with declining abilities, I now feel good about myself, am more energetic than I have been in years, and realize that I am in control of my continued success. My intrinsic desire for fitness success is fueled by the caring, personalized attention provided at Journey Fitness Coaching. Journey Fitness is a remarkable place that is inspiring others to improve their lives, and I am grateful they helped me change mine.

I am living proof that Journey Fitness Coaching is a 'top shelf' personal training center. I am such a raving fan of Journey Fitness that I decided in my retirement from a career in law enforcement

that I would apply for an internship at Journey Fitness. I was accepted as an intern and began their curriculum of learning all that I needed to know to be an effective fitness coach. I passed the final exam and now help out part-time at Journey Fitness. I am so grateful for the accomplishments I achieved, which would not have been possible without Journey Fitness. It now gives me great pleasure to help others progress towards their goals in the same way that the team at Journey Fitness helped me achieve mine.

The Journey Continues

I t's the journey of life. We all start in different places at different times and have different struggles, but by design our paths are meant to cross with others. Also by design, we are meant to struggle. We are meant to be tested and purified like gold. Today's failures become tomorrow's success as long as we recognize the error of our ways. Although I spent almost a decade in prison I would not ask to change that. It was through that struggle that God changed me and made me the man I am today.

Prior to prison I had fallen away from fitness and was not living the life God had created me to live. I feel like God used prison to help me re-discover my passion and bring the best out of me. I was not even a reader when I went to prison, yet today I am a multiple graduate and teacher. I was not a speaker and today I speak to groups frequently. I am a better father, husband and friend. My pain is the best part of who I am.

Our Journey continues to cross the paths of others. Journey Fitness grew in less than 2 years to over 350 clients, expanding into the former Curves location. We also opened a second Journey Fitness in Corning NY and we were voted Best New Business of The Year by the 700 members of the Chamber of Commerce. The people of Journey Fitness have lost over 9,000 lbs as a community. Our team now has grown to 15 employees. We continue to get 75% of our business from referrals, because we take care of our clients. We don't miss a month without doing some sort of fitness challenge outside of the normal training sessions, and we still track you down if you don't show up. Our team of coaches has grown, but we train them well and reproduce ourselves in each coach so the experience for our clients remains the same.

I believe that even coaches need coaches, and today my coach and mentor is Todd Durkin. Todd is a world renowned fitness trainer and entrepreneur. It's been said that the greatness we see in others is the greatness we see in ourselves. I love Todd's passion, his ability to inspire and his drive. I first connected with Todd when I heard him speak at a conference. I knew when I started my own business that he would be the best mentor to help me grow. I sought Todd out and applied to be in his group called the Power of 10. The Power of 10 is a group of fitness entrepreneurs focused on success and impacting the world of fitness, sharing their journey along the way for the betterment of the group. Ken Blanchard once wrote, "You are the average of the 5 people you hang out with." I would be proud to be the average of this group. It is because of this group that I went to California for a speaking engagement, authored this book, and am now teaching other fitness entrepreneurs to have the customer care business systems that Journey Fitness employs.

You may be wondering if I ever had any more God encounters. My most recent encounter with God happened when I started mentoring under Todd. It had been a while since we had been to church or taken time out for God. We were a family without a church because we had left the church of our former employer, and we were extremely busy starting our new business. I believe busy is one of the best tools the devil has to take us away from God. Despite the fact that I would walk through the Hair Hut Salon daily to do our fitness center's laundry, and while passing through that salon would hear Christian music playing and observe Bible scriptures on the wall, I still did not hear the voice of God. My daughter would spend time in the Salon, specifically with a special lady, Diane Mastrantonio. Diane did nails in the salon and one day Diane stopped me as I was traveling through to do the laundry. She said, "Travis. You think you are here for Journey Fitness, but you are actually here for your daughter Destiny and your family to grow closer to God." I remember thinking, "Oh Really! This lady thinks God talks to her about me and my family." Eventually I realized that yes, somewhere in the midst of getting so busy, I had forgotten how God helped me start Journey Fitness.

One day Cyndy, Destiny and I were riding in the car. My wife would drive when we took trips so I could work on the computer. I was a workaholic, and both my wife and daughter had learned to put up with it. Because I felt guilty about working so hard, I decided to involve them in an assignment Todd had sent me. Todd had sent homework called 'The Annual Strategic Roadmap' where I was supposed to answer a multitude of questions and set my goals for the New Year. I would answer each question according to our business goals, and then I would ask Cyndy and Destiny to answer personally. I got to the question, "What are three things you want to accomplish this year?" We all took turns, and when it got to my daughter she said, "I want to get baptized, read the Bible and go on a missions trip." We were shocked by her answer since we hadn't been going to church. Still, we were grateful at what an encouraging influence Diane Mastrantonio had been on our daughter and we felt accountable to help our daughter achieve her goals. When we returned from our trip we thanked Diane for the positive influence she had been on our daughter and asked if she had any recommendations on where we might start going to church. She recommended Maranatha Bible Church saying, "They do baptisms, take mission trips and are a good, Bible based, church."

We went to Maranatha Bible Church and found what Diane said to be true. I would say coincidentally, but I stopped believing in coincidence a long time ago and I have faith that, as God would have it, they were playing my favorite Christian song when we walked through the door. We felt very much welcome and at home in the church, so we inquired about both baptism and the mission. The church does a few baptism services per year and they were scheduled to conduct one the following week. The church supports a mission trip every 3 years and they were planning to send some members on one in 6 months. The group to deploy had already been formed and had commenced fund raising, but they said they would let us join in if we wanted to go. Destiny was baptized and we signed on to accompany the mission's trip.

The mission trip was going to cost about $1,500 per person. Neither my wife nor I wanted to let Destiny, at 12 years old, go alone yet we both didn't like the idea of needing to raise $4,500 to go to a third world, disease infested country where we would sleep in 100 degree heat without air conditioning and not even have the benefit of regular sewer and water. Still we loved our daughter and we wanted to do this for her, hoping that it would change her life and have a positive impact on her, to help shape her future in a positive way. We worked on our fundraising, hosting a few dinners to raise the necessary funds. As the day to leave drew closer, none of us wanted to go. As a family we went away often on weekends, so we missed church often as well. This meant that we hadn't gotten very close with the people that we would be traveling with to El Salvador. Our family was dreading the trip. Destiny did not want to leave her friends, Cyndy didn't want to live in the circumstances of El Salvador and I did not want to leave our business. In the end, the reason that we all went was because we owed it to the people who came out to support our fundraising dinners.

We arrived in El Salvador to 95 degree heat and instructions not to drink the water or flush our tissue paper down the toilet. Our mission groups were separated into men's and women's sections. Our sleeping quarters were triple stacked bunk beds which reminded me of prison. Worst of all for me was that I did not have my iPhone or my laptop. I was going to have to let go of work for a week. The strangest thing about the place was the missionaries that were hosting us. The missionaries were so happy! I had only been in El Salvador for a few hours, but that was long enough to know that they did not have a lot to be happy about. These missionaries were there for years and I was just trying to figure out how to make it through a week.

However, the week was well planned and well-orchestrated. We would be serving a branch of Envision Wired led by Ricardo Mullinax. Our group leaders were Daniel, Melissa, Tony and Nestor. We had a cook named Gloria and two translators named Pricilla and Hamilton. Our first day consisted of getting acquainted with El Salvador, so we traveled the streets with our translator Hamilton, being given certain tasks like feeding and praying for the homeless. After feeding a homeless man, Hamilton asked for one of us to offer prayer and we all realized how ill equipped we were to pray for the homeless, as none of us spoke much Spanish.

Since we landed in El Salvador, I had been using the broken Spanish I had learned while in prison and that made me the best choice when it came time for one of us to offer prayer for the homeless man. As I stepped forward to offer prayer, I had a flashback to a prison cell where a Mexican gang member who had found God told me how to ask in Spanish if someone knew Jesus. So, I said to the homeless man, "¿Conoces a Jesucristo" (Do you know Jesus?). The little, old and very dirty homeless man smiled and nodded, and then explained to me gesticulating in a way so that I would understand that he did know Jesus, but that he drank too much and so he sleeps on the street. Before we left we made a circle around the man and I prayed for him in English. What was amazing was that I could tell he felt very blessed, and that the prayer was just as good to him as it would have been in Spanish. I went to the mission feeling fulfilled, knowing that the homeless man saw God's love through me.

Every day that followed was more amazing than the previous. We broke into small groups to work on construction projects, and I was paired up with the youth pastor, Pastor Eric. As Pastor Eric and I worked together, he talked to me about the youth group at Maranatha and how it would be good for Destiny to join it, and for Cyndy and I to help out as youth group leaders. When he first told me about this, I didn't see how I would have time. Looking back, I see it as God inviting me to work with youth again. Pastor Eric told me we were going to be administering a vacation Bible School for the underprivileged children of El Salvador, and he asked me if I had any ideas for fitness events that we could include. I thought of several fun ways to incorporate fitness challenges, and for 3 days we visited the group and I led a daily fitness challenge, while Pastor Eric delivered a daily message about God. I never thought that when we went to El Salvador there would be a need for my fitness expertise. Oh how wrong I was.

One missionary had a back problem and asked me for stretches. Another missionary asked me for a program that he could do to get in shape. Then I was invited to the home of head missionary Ricardo Mullinax. Ricardo was about to turn 40 and he wanted  to get in shape before his birthday. He and his wife Jen had two children, named Alton and Arrow, and his boys had limited opportunities to participate in sports and fitness activities in El Salvador. Ricardo asked if I could come up with a workout that they could do together, one that would also help his boys to improve their basic athletic ability. I was very happy to do this, and much happier than I was helping with construction projects because, to be honest, I am terrible at most construction related things. I was able to have a couple of training sessions with Ricardo and his family, and I also held a couple of training sessions with some of the other missionaries.

By the end of our time in El Salvador, I led a shotgun guard bootcamp in the park attended by some members of our church group and some of the missionaries. In case you are wondering, a shotgun guard bootcamp is just what it sounds like. El Salvador is a dangerous place, and the mission has its own guard with a shotgun. We were not permitted to leave the mission by ourselves, so it took some convincing when I asked if we could all go across the street to the park to hold a bootcamp. Luckily for us, my exercise programs were earning positive reviews, so the guard was asked to keep watch on us while I hosted my first El Salvadoran bootcamp. I think this was the first time the park was used for this type of event. Typically, it is where homeless people sleep and drink.

It was amazing how God had turned my passion for fitness into a ministry in El Salvador. I felt like I could hear God saying to me that he had put these good desires in my heart for his purpose. I felt guilty knowing all that God had brought me through, and that I had been too busy for him. I was not the only one feeling guilty. Destiny and Cyndy had also come closer to God on this trip and we were changed as a fam-ily. We started the trip as a family barely going to church, and when we did go we considered it an inconvenience. When we first left for El Salvador we were leaving with a group of strangers. Now we were leaving El Salvador a family touched by God, feeling a part of a church family, and were excited about going to church.

Just before leaving El Salvador the children wanted to give us a gift that they made with their own hands. They gave us little wooden houses and told us they thought we were angels sent by God. I told them with tears in my eyes how much that touched my heart, and that they had given me much more than I could ever give them. The top of the wooden house was made to flip open and the children  asked what I would put inside. I told them that is where I would save money to come back someday.

On our plane ride home we arrived in Atlanta for our connection on an overbooked flight. The airline was asking for 3 volunteers to give up their seats, for which they each would be compensated with $500 vouchers. We decided to do it. When we approached the desk and offered our seats, the Delta agent asked what we had been doing in El Salvador and we told her we were on a mission's trip. She said, "On that note, I am going to give you $600 each." We arrived home a day later, all feeling overwhelmed by how the trip had changed each of our hearts, bringing us closer to God. We decided we would look up the cost of a plane ticket back. It was $598 for each of us. You might call it coincidence. I call it divine intervention. We booked our reservations to go back to El Salvador.

God has remained a part of my fitness activities. The first thing I did when I got home was pack up some fitness equipment and send it to El Salvador. I have not missed a week since, recording and sending an instructional workout video to augment the exercise equipment I sent to the missionaries. Ricardo is now down almost 40 pounds! The next thing we did is to start using our monthly fitness challenges to better help our community. One example of this is when we raised $5,000 for a member whose husband has ALS. I realized that you don't have to be in El Salvador to be on a mission.

Each day there is a mission field before us and it starts with each training client that we have the opportunity to help.

PASSAGES AUTHORED BY LEE BERRETTINI

The Origin of the "the ideal human diet?" started in the late 1990s. Over a 3 - 4 year time period, I attended several conferences across the U.S. and met with, or listened to presentations by, medical doctors who were treating and curing their patients with nutritional programs. This meant they were rarely using drug therapy, as drugs, with the exception of antibiotics, are not able to cure health ailments. They are designed to treat symptoms or manipulate biochemical pathways to produce a desired result, for example, to lower one's blood sugar or blood pressure. Functional or nutritional medicine, in contrast, attempts to support the body's ability to heal itself, and this ability is significant and powerful, especially if the body is fueled properly.

The doctors I met had varied practices; psychiatry, endocrinology, cardiology, gastroenterology, family practice, OB/GYN, and a PhD in Human Nutrition. I took what I believed were their best ideas, eliminated offending foods (grains, dairy protein, most fruit and excessive carbohydrates) in the recovery phase of what we were helping patients overcome. The diet was developed specifically to reverse compromised adrenal systems, but as I used it in that patient population, over the course of 5-6 months, we were noticing patients, in addition to recovering adrenal health, were no longer needing most or all of their prescriptions.

Today, we use it as the foundation in all patients who have complaints and there are times when that is all that is needed, sometimes without the need for targeted nutrients.

Although the diet looks and sounds strict, it quickly becomes easy because as you get metabolic balance (low, steady levels of blood sugar and insulin), there is no longer a biochemical reason for hunger or cravings, which are caused by fluctuations in blood sugar and insulin. That fluctuation begins a cascade of hormone disruption and fluctuations throughout the body as cortisol is disturbed, causing adrenal, thyroid, sex steroids, brain neurotransmitters, gut hormones, etc., to be influenced.

To experience the benefits of the diet, it must be adhered to - it cannot be done intermittently because it will be difficult or impossible to obtain and maintain metabolic balance.

BERT'S PHARMACY

WE ARE LEADING YOU TOWARD

AN IDEAL HUMAN DIET

The following is a description of what I believe to be the ideal human diet: it has moderate amounts of quality animal protein, high fiber, good fats and a low glycemic load. We have used it in many hundreds of patients to aid in hormone balancing, to reduce or eliminate drug therapy, to reduce inflammation, normalize blood pressure, blood sugar, treat various gut issues, etc. It has anti-inflammatory, anti-aging and anti-allergenic properties. It can best be described by using the image of your hand. Five fingers equate to 5 evenly spaced meals and/or snacks. Most often, three meals and two to three snacks are employed, and there should be a minimum of three evenly spaced meals. Snacks consist of whole foods only, for example, quality nuts like almonds, pecans or walnuts (keep in mind peanuts are NOT nuts, they are legumes and are not included), avocados, olives, sardines, anchovies or tuna in olive oil, raw vegetables like broccoli, cauliflower or celery, or hard-boiled or deviled eggs. Whey protein shakes (no soy protein) or low-carb, whey protein bars (no soy protein) can be good snacks or meal replacements. For the evenly spaced meals, the protein portion is the size of the palm of your hand and includes any quality animal protein; chicken, fish, eggs, red meat, etc. Ideally you would vary your sources of protein because you get different nutrients from different sources. For example, red meat is our primary source of carnitine, co-enzyme Q10, and vitamin B12. Also ideally, these protein sources would come from organically raised and fed animals. In the case of red meat, the animals should be grass/pasture fed, NOT grain-fed; in the case of poultry and eggs, these products should come from animals that are free-range, NOT grain-fed. The rest of your plate is filled with raw or lightly steamed vegetables; green, leafy vegetables like you'd find in a salad, or dense, fibrous, non-starchy vegetables like broccoli, cauliflower, green beans, asparagus, brussels sprouts, cabbage, spinach, etc. Lastly, a good neutral fat is put on the vegetables, like extra-virgin olive oil, avocado oil or organic butter. Do not be afraid of butter or other saturated fats as long as they are pure. Saturated fats have anti-microbial and anti-cancer properties, they are needed for hormone production, are the preferred foods for your heart and brain and there has never been any saturated fat found in arterial plaque. Items to avoid / eliminate on this eating plan include:

1. All grains (bread, pasta, cereal, crackers, and pretzels, anything made from wheat, flour, rice, oats, or corn).

2. Dairy, other than butter and / or real yogurt like original formula Stonyfield Farms or yogurt made from scratch from an active culture with no sweetener or fruit added.

3. Fruit (at least initially for glycemic control) later moderate amounts of low-sugar, high-fiber fruits like berries and cherries, etc. may be added in patients where glycemic control is not critical.

4. All vegetable oils need to be eliminated since they all contain trans-fats, and any fat that has been altered by man (corn, canola, soybean oil, margarines, etc.). For great information on fats and general nutritional needs, refer to www.westonaprice.org.

5. Caffeine should be eliminated or reduced as it can lead to insulin resistance and can cause certain hormones to fluctuate.

6. Lastly, all soy foods and soy supplements should be eliminated since soy can be damaging to our endocrine system (especially thyroid), can inhibit the absorption of key minerals (calcium, magnesium, zinc, copper and iron) and is associated with a higher incidence of some very deadly

digestive cancers (stomach, liver, esophageal and pancreatic), etc.

Refer again to the Weston Price website for a more thorough discussion of this. The above described eating plan is a whole foods diet. Humans need to avoid processed foods at all times if possible for many reasons.

Processed foods have been at least partially denuded of their natural nutrients, and chemicals like preservatives, flavor enhancers, coloring agents, etc. have been added. Other reasons to avoid processed foods are more insidious – anything that has been commercially baked or fried contains trans fats that are at the very least inflammatory and have been associated with heart disease and cancers for over 70 years. Also, the food industry has been including soy protein in many prepared foodstuffs either as a supposed quality source of protein (which it's not) or as cheap filler. Often soy itself is not mentioned as the source of protein but may be referred to as enriched flour, protein isolate, protein hydrosylate, vegetable broth, vegetable protein, etc. The message is to AVOID processed foods.

This diet / eating plan has been helpful in balancing adrenal function, reducing or eliminating the need for drugs to treat acid reflux, colitis, hypertension, hypercholesterolemia, non-insulin dependent diabetes, arthritis (both rheumatoid and osteoarthritis), asthma and allergies, sleep disorders, depression, etc., either by itself or in conjunction with targeted nutritional support. This eating plan may sound restrictive, but if adhered to, it will quickly lead to metabolic balance (low, steady levels of blood sugar and insulin).

When you achieve metabolic balance there is no biochemical reason to be hungry or have cravings. You cannot cheat on this eating plan and obtain or maintain metabolic balance. Experience has shown that with metabolic balance, the recovery phase in chronic, degenerative conditions can be one-fourth or less than the recovery phase without metabolic balance. Intelligent, sensible eating is critical and without it, recovery is at best delayed and at worst, impossible.

CAUTION: This is for educational or informational use only and not to treat any disease. If you are diabetic and on medication to treat that condition, do not start this eating plan unless you thoroughly understand your condition AND are working closely with a knowledgeable health care practitioner. ALWAYS consult with a knowledgeable health care practitioner whenever you consider dietary changes.

Lee Berrettini, R. Ph.

ABOUT THE AUTHOR

TRAVIS BARNES

 Travis Barnes is coauthor of the bestselling book 'Results Fitness' with Rachel and Alwyn Cosgrove and is also the author of his own book, 'Journey Fitness'. He has 20 years of experience in the fitness industry and has worked in all areas of fitness, including working as a group instructor, personal coach, program director, program designer, manager, and Chief Operations Officer. He is a certified trainer through the American Counsel of Exercise and with his wife Cyndy, currently owns and operates two personal training centers with the goal to grow to three within the next year. Travis then plans on franchising his systematic business model across the country. Travis Barnes is a real life example of how you can hit rock bottom, only to rise to the top.

Made in the USA
Middletown, DE
03 July 2015